2023 EDITIO

THE LOW-FODMAP

DIET COOKBOOK FOR BEGINNERS

Table of Contents

INTRODUCTION

The FODMAP diet has gained increasing recognition as an effective approach for managing gastrointestinal symptoms, particularly for individuals with conditions such as irritable bowel syndrome (IBS) and other functional gastrointestinal disorders. This book serves as a comprehensive guide, providing all the necessary information and practical tips to successfully implement and navigate the FODMAP diet.

Chapter by chapter, we will delve into the key aspects of the FODMAP diet, starting with an in-depth understanding of FODMAPs themselves. We will explore the science behind FODMAPs, their impact on the digestive system, and how they can trigger symptoms like bloating, gas, abdominal pain, and irregular bowel movements.

Moving forward, we will dive into the low-FODMAP diet, the central focus of this book. We will explore the principles of the diet, outlining which foods to include and avoid during the elimination phase. We will also discuss the benefits of following a low-FODMAP diet, including the potential reduction in gastrointestinal symptoms and improvements in overall well-being.

Understanding that a balanced approach is key, a chapter is dedicated to the high-FODMAP diet, outlining the types of foods that are rich in FODMAPs and their potential effects on the digestive system. By exploring the high-FODMAP diet, readers gain valuable knowledge on foods to avoid and the rationale behind their exclusion during the elimination phase.

Putting theory into practice, there are food recommendations for both the low-FODMAP and high-FODMAP diets. Most especially, readers will find a variety of recipes and meal ideas to help them get started on their low-FODMAP journey.

To ensure a seamless transition, we delve into the practical aspects of putting the low-FODMAP diet into practice. From creating a FODMAP-friendly kitchen to understanding food labels and dining out strategies, we equip readers with the tools they need to navigate everyday challenges while following the diet.

Throughout the book, there are emphasis on the importance of seeking guidance from a registered dietitian specializing in the FODMAP diet. Their expertise is invaluable in developing an individualized plan, monitoring nutrient intake, and ensuring long-term success.

Whether you're newly diagnosed with a digestive disorder or looking to better manage your symptoms, this book aims to empower you with knowledge and practical strategies to implement the FODMAP diet effectively. By taking a step-by-step approach and understanding the nuances of this dietary approach, you'll be well-equipped to regain control of your digestive health and improve your overall quality of life.

BOOK 1

CHAPTER ONE

All you need to know about FODMAP

What are FODMAP?

The symptoms caused by FODMAPs include bloating, abdominal pain, gas, abdominal distention, diarrhea, and other gastrointestinal issues. FODMAPs are forms of carbohydrates and sugar alcohols that are not absorbed effectively in the body.

These can be naturally present in foods or as supplements and can be found in artificial sweeteners, certain vegetables and fruits, dairy products containing lactose, high fructose corn syrup, beans, wheat, and lentils. They can also be found in artificially sweetened beverages.

Although most diets high in FODMAPs are nutritious and useful to the body, the reaction that some people have to these foods can be unpleasant.

People who suffer from gastrointestinal conditions such as irritable bowel syndrome (IBS), inflammatory bowel disease (IBD), gastroesophageal reflux disease (GERD), celiac disease, or diverticulitis can be adversely affected by foods that are high in FODMAPs.

Polyols, fructans, fructose, lactose, and galactans are the five types of FODMAPs that are most usually recognized. Sugar alcohols like xylitol, sorbitol, and mannitol are examples of polyols that can be found in some fruits and vegetables. Other examples include mannitol. Barley, spelt, rye, and other grains like wheat all include fructans, while legumes like lentils and beans have galactans. Table sugar, many fruits, vegetables, and added sugars all contain fructose, sometimes known as simple sugar. Fructose is also found in some added sugars. Last but not least, the primary source of carbohydrates in milk and other dairy products is lactose.

Fermentable Oligosaccharides, Disaccharides, Monosaccharides, and Polyols are what "FODMAP" stand for when they are combined into an acronym. These are the kinds of carbohydrates that are not well absorbed in the small intestine and are rapidly digested by bacteria in the large intestine, which might result in gas production as well as other symptoms.

The FODMAP

> **FERMENTABLE:** The breakdown of carbohydrates that occurs during fermentation is a process carried out by bacteria found in the intestines. The production of carbon dioxide (gas), hydrogen (gas), and/or methane (gas) in the colon is a natural and necessary part of the digestive process. It also enables the body to extract more vitamins, minerals, and energy from food. You read it correctly: we are talking about gas, gas, and even more gas. You may have symptoms such as bloating, abdominal pain, constipation, and diarrhea if the fermentation starts too quickly or if your body cannot absorb the by-products correctly.

> **OLIGOSACCHARIDES:** Even if they are short-chain carbs, you do not want to be a part of this buddy chain. Since this category encompasses three or more distinct kinds of sugar, its name was derived from the Greek for "a few sugars." Since the human body does not create enzymes that are capable of completely breaking down oligosaccharides, there is plenty of it for the bacteria in the intestines to ferment. This results in gas, pain, and other symptoms when there is too much of it. Oligosaccharides can be broken down into several types, two of which, fructans and galactans, are particularly troublesome. Wheat, rye, onions, and garlic are some foods that contain a significant amount of fructans. Pulses, such as lentils, beans, chickpeas, and soybeans, are foods rich in galactans.

➤ **DISACCHARIDES:** The word "disaccharides" comes from the prefix "di," which refers to the fact that there are two different kinds of sugars (saccharides) that are connected together. The disaccharide that you need to pay the most attention to is lactose, which is created by combining the monosaccharides galactose and glucose. It is necessary to have an enzyme known as "lactase" in order to break down this chain. Lactase production might decline with age or as a result of certain digestive problems, in addition to the fact that some persons do not generate any lactase at all. • Milk from cows, goats, and sheep all have naturally occurring lactose levels. Additionally, it can be found in dairy products such as ice cream, yogurt, and soft cheeses. Note that another kind of disaccharide is sucrose, which is created by combining glucose and fructose. If your body cannot create enough sucrase, the enzyme responsible for breaking down sugar, you may have bloating and gas as a result. The FODMAP diet does not place any restrictions on the consumption of sugar. If you do not get any relief after following the FODMAP diet plan, you may want to consider broaching the subject of a sucrase deficit with your primary care physician.

➤ **MONOSACCHARIDES**: The word "mono" in the term "monosaccharides" refers to the fact that this particular chain of carbohydrates contains only a single kind of sugar (saccharide), such as fructose or glucose. Fructose malabsorption can occur when a person consumes a disproportionately high amount of fructose in comparison to glucose in their diet. This indicates that the excessive fructose passes swiftly through the digestive tract without being absorbed as it should, leaving plenty for the bacteria in your stomach to ferment, which creates those uncomfortable and unpleasant sensations. Honey, mango, and high-fructose corn syrup are all examples of foods that contain significant levels of sugar fructose.

➢ **POLYOLS:** The small intestine is unable to absorb polyols, also called "sugar alcohols," due to the chemical composition of these compounds, which prevents their absorption. They travel through the digestive tract quite fast when consumed in high quantities, and as a result, they frequently result in diarrhea and cramping in the abdominal region. • Sorbitol, mannitol, maltitol, and xylitol are all included in this category of sugar alcohols. When you are out shopping and looking at labels on food, make sure you keep those "-itol" terms in mind. In this category, you'll find foods like avocados, plums, peaches, cauliflower, and certain sugar- or diet-friendly items. The fact that some foods contain more than one FODMAP makes it difficult to place all of those foods in the same category, as you would have guessed. Apples, pears, watermelons, sweet corn, and coconut flour are some of the food items that fall into this category.

CHAPTER TWO

The low-FODMAP diet

Irritable bowel syndrome is one of the symptoms that can be managed with a therapeutic diet called the Low FODMAP Diet (IBS). Irritable bowel syndrome (IBS) is a prevalent gastrointestinal condition estimated to affect 10-15% of the world's population. The patient may also have symptoms of abdominal pain, bloating, gas, constipation, or diarrhea. Research has indicated that particular kinds of carbohydrates, which are referred to as FODMAPs, can produce symptoms in certain people, even if the reasons for irritable bowel syndrome are not completely known.

The Low FODMAP Diet is a three-phase eradication diet that involves cutting high FODMAP foods from the daily intake for a period of time, followed by a gradual reintroduction of FODMAPs in order to identify trigger foods. This diet aims to reduce symptoms associated with irritable bowel syndrome (IBS). The diet's objective is to recognize and steer clear of items that set off allergic reactions while still consuming a nutritionally sound diet.

During the elimination phase, which lasts for four to six weeks, items that are rich in FODMAPs are eliminated from the diet. This category of foods includes wheat, onions, garlic, dairy products, beans, and specific fruits, including apples, cherries, and peaches, among others. Although some foods that are high in FODMAPs, like wheat, do contain gluten, a diet low in FODMAPs is not the same thing as a gluten-free diet.

After the elimination phase, FODMAPs are gradually reintroduced in a systematic manner, with one type of FODMAP introduced at a time. This helps to identify specific trigger foods and determine which FODMAPs can be tolerated in small amounts.

Once trigger foods have been identified, a personalized low FODMAP diet can be developed to manage symptoms while still maintaining a nutritionally balanced diet. It's important to note that the elimination phase is not intended to be long-term, and working with a registered dietitian is recommended to ensure that the diet is nutritionally balanced.

The maintenance phase involves creating a personalized, long-term diet that allows for adequate nutrient intake while minimizing high-FODMAP foods that trigger symptoms. This phase requires ongoing attention and adjustment to ensure that the diet remains effective in managing symptoms.

It's important to note that the low-FODMAP diet is not appropriate for everyone and should only be implemented under a healthcare provider's and registered dietitian's guidance. The diet may not be palatable for someone with certain medical conditions, such as celiac disease, and it may lead to nutrient deficiencies if not properly planned and monitored. Additionally, some individuals may find that other interventions, such as stress management or medication, are more effective in managing their symptoms.

While the low-FODMAP diet has been shown to be effective in reducing symptoms for many people with IBS and other gastrointestinal disorders, it's not a cure for these conditions. The diet is intended to manage symptoms and improve quality of life, but it's important to understand that it doesn't address the underlying cause of the condition.

Additionally, some people may find that a low-FODMAP diet is too restrictive or difficult to follow long-term. In these cases, other dietary interventions or treatments may be more appropriate. It's crucial to work with a well-trained healthcare provider and registered dietitian to determine the best course of action for managing symptoms.

It's also worth noting that research into the low-FODMAP diet is ongoing, and there is still much to learn about the diet's long-term safety and effectiveness. While the diet has been shown to be effective in reducing symptoms in the short-term, more research is needed to determine its safety and effectiveness over the long term.

CHAPTER THREE

The benefits of low-FODMAP Diet

The signs of irritable bowel syndrome (IBS) and other gastrointestinal illnesses have been proven to be relieved by following a diet that is low in FODMAPs.

Some of the benefits of the low-FODMAP diet include:

1. **Increased Nutrient Absorption:** By reducing digestive symptoms, the Low-FODMAP Diet can improve the absorption of nutrients from food. When high-FODMAP foods are poorly absorbed in the small intestine, they can contribute to the malabsorption of nutrients, leading to deficiencies in important vitamins and minerals. By eliminating high-FODMAP foods from the diet, individuals may experience improved nutrient absorption and therefore improved overall health and well-being.

2. **Improved Mood:** Research has shown that individuals with IBS are more likely to experience anxiety and depression. By reducing digestive symptoms, the Low-FODMAP Diet may improve mood and overall quality of life.

3. **Increased Dietary Variety:** While the Low-FODMAP diet does restrict certain foods, it also encourages the consumption of a wide variety of low-FODMAP foods. This can lead to a more varied and balanced diet.

4. **Improved Quality of Life:** By reducing digestive symptoms and improving overall health, the Low-FODMAP Diet can significantly improve the quality of life for individuals with IBS. This can lead to increased productivity, social engagement, and overall well-being.

Following a low-FODMAP diet has been shown to improve the quality of life in individuals with gastrointestinal disorders, such as irritable bowel syndrome (IBS). This is because the low-FODMAP diet can help reduce symptoms, such as bloating, gas, abdominal pain, and diarrhea or constipation.

When these symptoms are reduced, individuals may experience improved energy levels, better sleep, and reduced stress and anxiety related to their gastrointestinal symptoms. This can lead to an overall improvement in quality of life and ability to engage in daily activities.

It's important to note that the low-FODMAP diet is not intended to be a long-term diet but rather a temporary elimination and reintroduction of high-FODMAP foods to identify triggers and determine individual tolerance levels. Once triggers have been identified, a more balanced and varied diet can be implemented to ensure adequate nutrient intake.

5. **Reduction in gastrointestinal symptoms:** The low-FODMAP diet has been shown to be effective in reducing symptoms such as abdominal pain, bloating, gas, and diarrhea in individuals with IBS and other gastrointestinal disorders.

High-FODMAP foods are known to be poorly absorbed in the small intestine and can cause fermentation and gas production in the large intestine.

By eliminating high-FODMAP foods from the diet and then gradually reintroducing them, individuals can identify specific triggers that may be contributing to their symptoms. This can allow for a more targeted approach to managing symptoms and reducing the frequency and severity of gastrointestinal symptoms.

In addition to the elimination and reintroduction of high-FODMAP foods, a low-FODMAP diet may also involve other dietary modifications, such as increasing fiber intake, reducing fat intake, and avoiding certain foods that are known to trigger symptoms in some individuals.

6. **Personalized approach:** The reintroduction phase of the low-FODMAP diet allows for a personalized approach to managing symptoms, as it helps to identify individual tolerance levels for specific FODMAPs.

7. **Avoiding unnecessary restrictions:** The low-FODMAP diet allows for a more flexible approach to managing symptoms, as it does not require the unnecessary restriction of entire food groups, such as gluten or dairy.

It's important to note that the low-FODMAP diet is not appropriate for everyone and should only be implemented under the guidance of a healthcare provider and registered dietitian. Additionally, the diet should not be used long-term, as it may lead to nutrient deficiencies if not properly planned and monitored.

CHAPTER FOUR

Food Recommendations for low-FODMAP Diet

Vegetables

- ✓ lettuce

- ✓ alfalfa sprouts

- ✓ tomatoes

- ✓ ginger

- ✓ water chestnuts

- ✓ kale

- ✓ parsnips

- ✓ potatoes

- ✓ zucchini

- ✓ carrots

- ✓ olives

- ✓ green beans

- ✓ eggplant

- ✓ chives

- ✓ bell peppers

- ✓ radishes spinach

- ✓ green spring onions

- ✓ celery

- ✓ turnips

- ✓ bamboo shoots

- ✓ squash

- ✓ sweet potatoes

- ✓ bean sprouts

- ✓ cucumbers

- ✓ bok choy

Fresh fruit

- ✓ strawberries

- ✓ cantaloupes

- ✓ mandarins

- ✓ passionfruit

- ✓ raspberries

- ✓ blueberries

- ✓ lemons

- ✓ oranges

- ✓ grapefruit

- ✓ honeydew melons

- ✓ grapes

- ✓ lime

- ✓ oranges

- ✓ bananas

- ✓ kiwi

Dairy & Protein

- ✓ All meats and seafood (beef, fish, poultry)

- ✓ Lactose-free kefir

- ✓ Rice milk

- ✓ Tempeh

- ✓ Hard cheeses (including Cheddar, Colby, feta, mozzarella, Parmesan, and Swiss)

- ✓ Lactose-free dairy products

- ✓ Almond milk

- ✓ Coconut yogurt

- ✓ Eggs

✓ Tofu (soft or firm but not silken)

Grains & Starches

✓ Gluten-free white bread

✓ Grits

✓ Pasta made from corn, quinoa, or rice

✓ Corn chips

✓ Corn tortillas

✓ Rice (any variety)

✓ Rice crackers

✓ Polenta

✓ Popcorn

✓ Quinoa

Pulses And Nuts

✓ Flax seeds

✓ Pumpkin seeds (pepitas)

✓ Sunflower seeds

- ✓ Peanuts

- ✓ Almond butter

- ✓ Chia seeds

- ✓ Peanut butter

Pantry Staples

- ✓ Dark chocolate

- ✓ Ghee

- ✓ Gingerroot

- ✓ Avocado oil

- ✓ Mustard

- ✓ Olives

- ✓ Raw sugar

- ✓ Soy sauce

- ✓ Stevia

- ✓ Olive oil

- ✓ Brown rice syrup

- ✓ Butter

- ✓ Cacao powder

- ✓ Mayonnaise

Beverages

- ✓ Cranberry juice

- ✓ Gin

- ✓ Wine

- ✓ Vodka

- ✓ Black coffee

- ✓ Black, green, or white tea

- ✓ Certain herbal teas (such as ginger and peppermint)

- ✓ Whiskey

CHAPTER FIVE

The high-FODMAP Diet

High-FODMAP

The high-FODMAP diet is the opposite of the low-FODMAP diet and involves consuming foods that are high in FODMAPs. While high-FODMAP foods may not cause symptoms in individuals without gastrointestinal disorders, they can trigger symptoms in individuals with conditions such as IBS.

Consuming high-FODMAP foods can lead to symptoms such as bloating, abdominal pain, diarrhea, and gas in individuals with IBS and other gastrointestinal disorders.

It's important to note that not all high-FODMAP foods need to be completely avoided, and tolerance levels can vary between individuals.

While the high-FODMAP diet may not be suitable for individuals with gastrointestinal disorders, it may be appropriate for individuals without these conditions who do not experience symptoms after consuming high-FODMAP foods.

It's important to note that the high-FODMAP diet should not be used as a weight loss or "detox" diet, as it can lead to nutrient deficiencies if not properly planned and monitored. High-FODMAP foods, such as fruits and vegetables, are an important source of fiber, vitamins, and minerals, which are essential for overall health.

Additionally, avoiding high-FODMAP foods without medical necessity can lead to unnecessary food restrictions and anxiety around food, which can have negative effects on mental health and quality of life.

If you suspect that you have a gastrointestinal disorder, it's important to consult with a healthcare provider and registered dietitian to determine the appropriate course of action. In some cases, the low-FODMAP diet may be recommended as a tool to help manage symptoms, while in other cases, other dietary modifications or medical treatments may be necessary.

Effects of High-FODMAP

High-FODMAP foods can cause a variety of gastrointestinal symptoms in individuals with conditions such as IBS. Some of the disadvantages of consuming high-FODMAP foods include the following:

➢ Bloating:

Bloating is a common symptom experienced by someone with gastrointestinal disorders, such as IBS, after consuming high-FODMAP foods. Bloating is characterized by a sensation of fullness or tightness in the abdomen, often accompanied by visible swelling or distension.

Bloating can occur as a result of so many factors, including the buildup of gas in the gut, slowed digestion, and increased water retention in the gut. In individuals with gastrointestinal disorders, consuming high-FODMAP foods can exacerbate these factors and lead to bloating.

The low-FODMAP diet may be recommended to manage bloating associated with high-FODMAP foods. This diet involves eliminating high-FODMAP foods for a period of time to allow the gut to heal and then systematically reintroducing them to determine individual tolerance levels.

In addition to dietary modifications, other strategies to manage bloating may include staying well-hydrated, eating smaller, more frequent meals, avoiding carbonated beverages, and practicing stress-reduction techniques such as meditation or yoga.

➤ Abdominal pain:

Abdominal pain is another common symptom experienced by individuals with gastrointestinal disorders, such as IBS, after consuming high-FODMAP foods. Abdominal pain is characterized by discomfort or pain in the abdominal region, which can range from mild to severe.

Abdominal pain can occur due to factors such as the buildup of gas in the gut, inflammation, and muscle contractions in the intestines. In individuals with gastrointestinal disorders, consuming high-FODMAP foods can exacerbate these factors and lead to abdominal pain.

Following a low-FODMAP diet may be suggested to alleviate stomach discomfort brought on by eating foods rich in FODMAPs. This diet involves eliminating high-FODMAP foods for a period to allow the gut to heal and then systematically reintroduce them to determine individual tolerance levels.

In addition to dietary modifications, other strategies to manage abdominal pain may include the use of medications such as antispasmodics or pain relievers, stress-reduction techniques such as meditation or yoga, and regular exercise.

➤ Diarrhea:

Diarrhea is a common symptom experienced by individuals with gastrointestinal disorders, such as IBS, after consuming high-FODMAP foods. Diarrhea is characterized by loose, watery stools and an increased frequency of bowel movements.

Diarrhea can be caused by a variety of factors, including increased fluid secretion in the gut, increased gut motility, and changes in gut bacteria. In individuals with gastrointestinal disorders, consuming high-FODMAP foods can exacerbate these factors and lead to diarrhea.

The low-FODMAP diet is often suggested as a treatment option for managing diarrhea that may be caused by meals that are rich in FODMAPs. This diet involves eliminating high-FODMAP foods for a period of time to allow the gut to heal and then systematically reintroducing them to determine individual tolerance levels.

In addition to dietary modifications, other strategies to manage diarrhea may include staying well-hydrated, consuming low-fiber foods, avoiding high-fat or spicy foods, and consuming probiotics or other supplements to improve gut bacteria balance.

➢ Constipation:

Constipation is a common gastrointestinal symptom that can be caused by a variety of factors, including a lack of fiber in the diet, dehydration, lack of physical activity, certain medications, and changes in gut bacteria. The low-FODMAP diet has been found to be effective in managing constipation in individuals with gastrointestinal disorders, such as irritable bowel syndrome (IBS).

The low-FODMAP diet involves eliminating high-FODMAP foods for a period of time to allow the gut to heal and then systematically reintroducing them to determine individual tolerance levels. This can help identify specific foods that may be contributing to constipation.

In addition to dietary modifications, there are several lifestyle changes that can help manage constipation. These include increasing fiber intake (particularly soluble fiber), drinking plenty of fluids, engaging in regular physical activity, managing stress, and avoiding certain medications that can contribute to constipation.

If constipation persists despite dietary and lifestyle changes, it's important to consult with a healthcare provider to rule out any underlying medical conditions that may be contributing to the problem. In some cases, additional medical testing or treatments may be necessary to address the underlying causes of constipation.

➢ Nutrient deficiencies:

Consuming a high-FODMAP diet may contribute to nutrient deficiencies in some individuals. This is because many high-FODMAP foods are also important sources of key vitamins and minerals, such as fiber, vitamin C, and potassium.

For example, individuals who follow a strict low-FODMAP diet may limit their intake of fruits and vegetables, which are typically high in fiber and important vitamins and minerals. This can lead to deficiencies in these nutrients if adequate substitutions are not made.

To prevent nutrient deficiencies while following a low-FODMAP diet, it's important to choose nutrient-dense, low-FODMAP foods, such as leafy greens, berries, nuts, and seeds. In some cases, a registered dietitian may recommend supplementation with key nutrients to ensure adequate intake.

It's important to note that nutrient deficiencies are not limited to those following a low-FODMAP diet and can occur in individuals with gastrointestinal disorders, such as IBS, regardless of their diet.

All high-FODMAP foods will cause symptoms in every individual with gastrointestinal disorders, and tolerance levels can vary between individuals. The low-FODMAP diet involves identifying individual tolerance levels for specific FODMAPs and reintroducing high-FODMAP foods in a systematic way to determine which ones can be tolerated without causing symptoms.

CHAPTER SIX

Foods to avoid (High-FODMAP Diet)

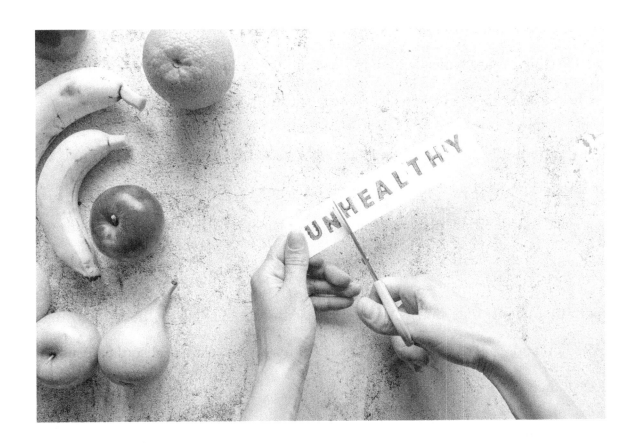

Dairy & Protein

- ✓ Evaporated milk

- ✓ Frozen yogurt

- ✓ Soft, unripened cheeses (cream cheese, cottage cheese, mascarpone, ricotta)

- ✓ Soy milk

- ✓ Yogurt

- ✓ Buttermilk

- ✓ Condensed milk

- ✓ Custard

- ✓ Dry powdered milk

- ✓ Ice cream

- ✓ Milk from cows, goats, and sheep

Fruits

- ✓ Avocados

- ✓ Blackberries

- ✓ Apples (including apple juice, apple cider, and applesauce)

- ✓ Apricots

- ✓ Plums

- ✓ Watermelon

- ✓ Cherries

- ✓ Nectarines

- ✓ Peaches

- ✓ Pears (including pear juice)

- ✓ Dried fruits (including dried fruit juices)

- ✓ Mangos

- ✓ Pomegranate

Vegetables

- ✓ Beets

- ✓ Garlic

- ✓ Green peas

- ✓ Leeks

- ✓ Brussels sprouts

- ✓ Snow peas

- ✓ Sugar snap peas

- ✓ Sweet corn

- ✓ Cabbage (savoy)

- ✓ Radicchio

- ✓ Scallion bulbs

- ✓ Artichokes

- ✓ Asparagus

- ✓ Cauliflower

- ✓ Mushrooms

- ✓ Onions

- ✓ Pumpkin

- ✓ Shallots

Grains & Starches

- ✓ Spelt

- ✓ Wheat and derivatives

- ✓ Coconut flour

- ✓ Couscous

- ✓ Gnocchi (from wheat)

- ✓ Barley

- ✓ Bread

- ✓ Oatmeal

- ✓ Rye

Pulses And Nuts

- ✓ Pistachios

- ✓ Silken tofu

- ✓ Chickpeas (garbanzo beans)

- ✓ Veggie burgers (containing soy and beans)

- ✓ Lentils

- ✓ Beans

- ✓ Cashews

Pantry Staples

- ✓ Molasses

- ✓ Pancake syrup

- ✓ Crystalline fructose

- ✓ High-fructose corn syrup

- ✓ Agave nectar

- ✓ Agave syrup

- ✓ Honey

Beverages

- ✓ Chai

- ✓ Eggnog

- ✓ Carob powder

- ✓ Certain herbal teas (chamomile, fennel, oolong)

- ✓ Rum

CHAPTER SEVEN

Putting the Low Fodmap Diet into Practice

Implementing a low-FODMAP diet can be challenging, but with some planning and guidance, it can be done successfully. Here are some tips for putting the low-FODMAP diet into practice:

1. **Seek guidance from a registered dietitian:**

Working with a registered dietitian who is knowledgeable about the low-FODMAP diet can be invaluable in developing an individualized plan and ensuring that all nutrient needs are met.

Working with a registered dietitian (RD) who is trained in the low-FODMAP diet can be an essential part of successfully implementing this dietary approach. An RD can provide individualized guidance on how to follow the diet while ensuring that all nutrient needs are met.

When seeking a registered dietitian, it's important to look for someone who is experienced and knowledgeable in the low-FODMAP diet. They should also have a good understanding of digestive disorders and be able to provide support throughout the elimination and reintroduction phases.

An RD can help with:

o Creating a customized meal plan: An RD can help create a customized meal plan based on individual needs and preferences, ensuring that all nutrient needs are met while avoiding high-FODMAP foods.

o Providing education on the low-FODMAP diet: An RD can provide education on the low-FODMAP diet, including which foods are high in FODMAPs and how to read food labels.

o Identifying trigger foods: An RD can help identify trigger foods and advise on appropriate substitutions, as well as help to gradually reintroduce high-FODMAP foods to determine individual tolerance levels.

- Providing support and accountability: An RD can provide ongoing support and accountability, helping individuals to stay on track and make adjustments as needed.

Working with an RD can help to ensure that the low-FODMAP diet is implemented safely and effectively while minimizing the risk of nutrient deficiencies and other negative health outcomes.

2. Start with a FODMAP elimination phase:

The first phase of the low-FODMAP diet involves eliminating high-FODMAP foods from the diet for a period of 4-6 weeks. During this time, it's important to focus on low-FODMAP foods to ensure adequate nutrient intake.

It's important to note that the elimination phase should only be done under the guidance of a healthcare professional, such as a registered dietitian, to ensure that all nutrient needs are met and to monitor for any potential side effects.

The elimination phase involves removing foods that are high in certain types of carbohydrates, including:

- Fructose: Fructose is readily found in fruits such as pears, apples, and mangoes, as well as sweeteners such as high-fructose corn syrup.

- Lactose: Found in dairy products such as milk, yogurt, and cheese.

- Fructans: Found in foods such as wheat, onions, and garlic.

- Galactans: Found in beans, lentils, and legumes.

o   Polyols: Found in some fruits such as cherries and plums, as well as sugar alcohols such as sorbitol and xylitol.

During the elimination phase, individuals should focus on consuming low-FODMAP foods, including:

o   Vegetables: such as carrots, spinach, zucchini, tomatoes, and bell peppers.

o   Fruits: such as bananas, blueberries, grapes, oranges, and strawberries.

o   Grains: such as rice, oats, quinoa, and gluten-free bread.

o   Proteins: such as chicken, fish, beef, and tofu.

o   Fats and oils: Oil such as olive oil, avocado, and coconut oil.

By following the elimination phase, individuals can begin to identify which FODMAPs trigger their symptoms, which will help them develop a long-term, sustainable, low-FODMAP diet that works for them.

3. Gradually reintroduce high-FODMAP foods:

After the elimination phase, the next step is to gradually reintroduce high-FODMAP foods back into the diet to determine which FODMAPs trigger symptoms and in what amounts. This phase should also be done under the guidance of a registered dietitian to ensure that the process is done safely and effectively.

The reintroduction phase involves systematically reintroducing one high-FODMAP food at a time in small amounts and monitoring any symptoms that occur over a period of two to three days. This allows individuals to identify which FODMAPs trigger their symptoms and in what amounts, allowing them to personalize their low-FODMAP diet.

It's important to note that not all high-FODMAP foods will trigger symptoms in all individuals. Some individuals may be able to tolerate certain high-FODMAP foods in small amounts, while others may need to avoid them completely.

Once an individual has identified their trigger foods, they can create a personalized low-FODMAP diet that includes a variety of low-FODMAP foods that they enjoy and are nutrient-dense.

4. Keep a food diary:

Keeping a food diary is an essential part of the low-FODMAP diet, especially during the elimination and reintroduction phases. A food diary allows individuals to track their food intake and symptoms and identify trigger foods.

During the elimination phase, it's recommended to keep a detailed food diary to track all food and drink consumed, including portion sizes and any symptoms experienced. This information can help individuals and their dietitians identify potential trigger foods.

During the reintroduction phase, it's important to continue keeping a food diary to track the reintroduction of high-FODMAP foods and any associated symptoms. This will help individuals identify which FODMAPs trigger symptoms and in what amounts.

When keeping a food diary, individuals should record the following information:

- o Food and drink consumed: including portion sizes and cooking methods.

- o Time of day: record the time the food was consumed.

- o Symptoms experienced: record any gastrointestinal symptoms experienced, such as bloating, abdominal pain, diarrhea, or constipation.

- o Other factors: record any other factors that may have contributed to symptoms, such as stress, lack of sleep, or exercise.

By keeping a food diary, individuals can work with their dietitian to identify patterns in their symptoms and make necessary adjustments to their diet to optimize symptom m

5. Experiment with low-FODMAP recipes:

Experimenting with low-FODMAP recipes is a great way to add variety and flavor to the low-FODMAP diet. It's crucial to remember that just because a food is low in FODMAPs, it doesn't mean it's not delicious or satisfying.

When experimenting with low-FODMAP recipes, individuals should focus on incorporating a variety of nutrient-dense foods that are low in FODMAPs. This includes fruits and vegetables such as carrots, cucumber, bell peppers, and strawberries, as well as lean proteins like chicken, fish, and tofu.

There are many low-FODMAP recipes available online and in cookbooks, including low-FODMAP versions of popular dishes such as lasagna, stir-fry, and chili. It's important to note that portion sizes and ingredient substitutions may need to be adjusted based on individual tolerance levels.

Some examples of low-FODMAP recipes include:

- o Low-FODMAP chicken and vegetable stir-fry with rice noodles

- o Low-FODMAP spaghetti with tomato and basil sauce

- o Low-FODMAP beef and vegetable chili

- o Low-FODMAP roasted salmon with lemon and herbs

- o Low-FODMAP vegetable frittata

By experimenting with low-FODMAP recipes, individuals can discover new and delicious meals that fit their dietary needs and preferences.

6. Be patient:

Being patient is an important aspect of putting the low-FODMAP diet into practice. The elimination and reintroduction phases can take several weeks to complete, and it may take some time to identify trigger foods and find a suitable long-term diet.

During the elimination phase, it's important to be patient and follow the diet strictly to ensure accurate results. It can be challenging to restrict certain foods and adjust to a new way of eating, but it's important to remember that it's only temporary.

During the reintroduction phase, it's important to reintroduce one high-FODMAP food at a time and allow for at least three days between each food to observe any symptoms. This process can be time-consuming, but it's essential to accurately identify trigger foods and develop a sustainable long-term diet.

Additionally, it's important to remember that the low-FODMAP diet is not a cure for gastrointestinal issues but rather a management tool. It may take some time to unveil the right balance of low-FODMAP and high-FODMAP foods that work for each individual, and it may require ongoing monitoring and adjustments.

By being patient and working closely with a registered dietitian, individuals can successfully implement the low-FODMAP diet and improve their gastrointestinal symptoms and overall quality of life.

By following these tips and working with a healthcare provider and registered dietitian, individuals can successfully implement a low-FODMAP diet to manage gastrointestinal symptoms and improve overall health and well-being.

BOOK 1

MEAL PLAN
AND RECIPES

CHAPTER ONE

MEAL PLAN

30-DAY MEAL PLAN

DAY	BREAKFAST	LUNCH	DINNER
1	On-the-Go Nutty Oats	Nutty Summer Fruit Salad	Wild Rice & Ginger Cod
2	Easy Breakfast Sausage	Mashed Potatoes	Greek-Style Lamb Skewers
3	Crunchy Granola	Lentil Chili	Pineapple Fried Rice
4	Quinoa Breakfast Bowl with Basil "hollandaise" Sauce	Brown Rice & Vegetable Bowl	Low-FODMAP Chicken Curry
5	Summer Berry Smoothie	Beef & Zucchini Stir-Fry	Cheese Strata
6	Protein Smoothie	Nutty Gluten-Free Pasta Salad	Quick Italian Herb Chicken
7	Pasta With Pesto Sauce	Bok Choy Tuna Salad	Mexican-Style Fish Wraps
8	Nourishing Basmati Rice Gruel	Turkey And Brown Rice Soup	Italian-Style Beef Casserole
9	Corn Salad	Low-FODMAP Toasted Tuna Sandwich	Tangy Ground Turkey Buns
10	Nutty Banana Smoothie	Nutty Chicken & Mustard Salad	Spicy Fried Shrimp & Bok Choy
11	Pineapple, Strawberry, Raspberry Smoothie	Butternut Salad with Pomegranate Seeds	Pan fried Tilapia with Olives

12	Spanish Rice	Spinach And Bell Pepper Salad With Fried Tofu Puffs	Dijon-roasted Pork Tenderloin
13	Basic Smoothie Base	Blue Cheese Bacon Salad	Vegetable Nori Roll
14	Coconut Cacao Hazelnut Smoothie Bowl	Caramelized Fennel	Chili-lime Shrimp And Bell Peppers
15	Turmeric Rice with Cranberries	Smoked Gouda And Tomato Sandwich	Beef Stir-fry with Chinese Broccoli And Green Beans
16	Green Smoothie	Glorious Strawberry Salad	Pan-seared Scallops with Sautéed Kale
17	Sausage And Egg Omelet	Hearty Vegetarian Lettuce Bowls	Creamy Smoked Salmon Pasta
18	Quiche In Ham Cups	Orange, Red, And Green Buckwheat Salad	Breaded Fish Fillets with Spicy Pepper Relish
19	Fruity Yogurt Protein-Packed Breakfast	Kale Sesame Salad with Tamari-ginger Dressing	Pasta With Pesto Sauce
20	Vegetable Stir-fry	French Salad with Mustard Dressing	Garden Veggie Dip Burgers
21	Pineapple Fried Rice	Easy Fruit Salad	Moroccan Fish Stew with Cod, Fennel, Potatoes, and Tomatoes
22	Strawberry-kiwi Smoothie with Chia Seeds	Abundantly Happy Kale Salad	Mixed Grains, Seeds, And Vegetable Bowl
23	Breakfast Wrap	Peppered Beef And Citrus Salad	Balsamic-glazed Salmon & Swiss Chard
24	Mexican Egg Brunch	Mashed Potatoes	Eggplant And Chickpea Curry
25	Chive-Topped Smoked Salmon Toast	Grilled Halibut with Lemony Pesto	Cumin Turkey With Fennel
26	Carrot And Walnut Salad	Chicken Noodle Soup with Bok Choy	Sautéed Shrimp With Cilantro-lime Rice
27	Peanut Butter Soba Noodles	Rita's Linguine with Clam Sauce	Italian-Style Pasta & Shrimp
28	Egg Wraps	Atlantic Cod With Basil Walnut Sauce	Grilled Cod with Fresh Basil
29	Sweet Green Smoothie	Chive Dip	Chicken And Rice With Peanut Sauce
30	Smoothie Bowl	Shrimp Puttanesca with Linguine	Pork And Fennel Meatballs

CHAPTER TWO

BREAKFAST RECIPES

On-the-Go Nutty Oats

Cooking Time: 0 Mins   Makes: 1 Serving
Ingredients:
½ tsp. ground cinnamon
1 ½ tsp. chia seeds
½ cup rolled oats
½ cup almond milk
¼ cup toasted almonds, chopped
1 tbsp. low-FODMAP protein powder
1 tbsp. pure maple syrup

Directions:
➢ Put all the necessary ingredients in a clean bowl and stir them until properly mixed.
➢ Pour the mixture into a glass jar and seal with a lid, then refrigerate overnight.
➢ Grab the oats to eat cold, or simply pop the jar into the microwave for a few minutes before eating.

Nutrition: Calories: 307, Carbohydrate: 54.8g, Protein: 10.7g, Fat: 5.3g

Nourishing Basmati Rice Gruel

Cooking Time: 20 Mins   Makes: 1 Serving
Ingredients:
2 tsp. ground cinnamon
⅓ tsp. ground nutmeg
2 tbsp. pure maple syrup
1 can unsweetened coconut milk
2 cups warm water
1 tsp. salt
1 cup basmati rice

Directions:
➢ Boil water in a medium pot before reducing the heat and stirring in the rice and salt.
➢ Let the rice simmer for 1 minute.

➢ Add the pure maple syrup, cinnamon, nutmeg, and unsweetened coconut milk.
➢ Cook the rice with the lid on the pot for roughly 20 minutes, stirring every few minutes.
➢ Remove the pot of rice from the stove when the rice is soft, and the water has been absorbed.
➢ Serve right away.

Nutrition: Calories: 283, Fat: 21g, Protein: 9g, Carbohydrates: 55.

Coconut Cacao Hazelnut Smoothie Bowl

Cooking Time: X   Servings:1
Ingredients:
5 hazelnuts, chopped
1 tablespoon pumpkin seeds
1 frozen medium banana
2 teaspoons raw unsweetened cacao powder
1 tablespoon shredded unsweetened coconut
1 cup unsweetened almond milk
1/2 tablespoon maple syrup
1/8 teaspoon sea salt
1/2 cup ice

Directions:
➢ Place coconut in a small skillet over medium heat, stirring frequently until flakes are golden brown, then set aside.
➢ Place cacao, maple syrup, milk, banana, and salt in a blender with ice and blend until smooth. You can add more ice if necessary to make the mixture thick and icy.
➢ Pour the mixture into a serving bowl and top with pumpkin seeds, hazelnuts, and toasted coconut.

Nutrition: Calories: 380, Fat: 15g, Protein: 13g, Carbohydrates: 54.

Nutty Banana Smoothie

Cooking Time: 0 Mins   Makes: 2 Servings
Ingredients:
2 tbsp. pecan butter
1 tsp. maple syrup
½ cup coconut milk
1 frozen, plantain
1 cup lactose free milk
⅓ tsp. pure vanilla extract

Directions:
➢ Place all of the necessary ingredients in a blender and blend on high speed until you have a lump-free smoothie.
➢ Pour the smoothie into a glass and serve.

Nutrition: Calories: 204, Fat: 9g, Protein: 12g, Carbohydrates: 18g

Fruity Yogurt Protein-Packed Breakfast

Cooking Time: 0 Mins   Makes: 1 Serving
Ingredients:
1 tbsp. toasted coconut
2 tbsp. rolled oats
1 tbsp. gluten-free, low-FODMAP protein powder
½ cup mixed berries (blueberries, raspberries, and strawberries)
1 ½ tsp. pure maple syrup
1 tbsp. almond butter
⅓ unripe banana
½ cup unsweetened coconut yogurt
1 tsp. chia seeds

Directions:
➢ Place the pure maple syrup, unripe banana, mixed berries, protein powder, almond butter, and coconut yogurt in a blender and blend on the highest setting for about 1 minute or until it forms a smooth fruity yogurt.
➢ Pour the fruity yogurt into a bowl and top with chia seeds, toasted coconut, and rolled oats.

Nutrition: Calories: 231, Fat: 3.5g, Protein: 20g, Carbohydrates: 30.

Chive-Topped Smoked Salmon Toast

Cooking Time:0 Mins   Makes: 1 Serving
Ingredients:
2 tbsp. lactose-free cream cheese
1 slice low-FODMAP or gluten-free bread
Kosher salt
Chopped fresh dill
½ tsp. dried chives
¼ tsp. garlic-infused oil
¾ oz. plain smoked salmon
Freshly ground black pepper

Directions:
➢ Combine the garlic-infused oil, dried chives, and
➢ cream cheese in a small bowl.
➢ Toast the bread.
➢ Spread the cream cheese mixture over the toast, then add the salmon.
➢ Sprinkle with pepper and salt before garnishing with fresh
➢ dill.

Nutrition: Calories: 121, Fat: 5.4g, Protein: 17g, Carbohydrates: 0g.

Smoothie Bowl

Cooking Time: 5 Mins **Servings:2**
Ingredients:
1 cup coconut yogurt
½ cup coconut milk, canned or fresh
4 bananas, cut into slices and frozen
2 cups frozen mixed berries
2 tsp lemon juice
½ cup mixed nuts, chopped
2 mint leaves, torn

Directions:
➤ Mix frozen berries, yogurt, milk, bananas, and lemon juice in a blender.
➤ Pour the mixture into bowls and top with nuts and mint.

Nutrition: Calories: 324g, Fat: 17g, Carbohydrates: 36g, Protein: 9g.

Summer Berry Smoothie

Cooking Time: X **Servings:4**
Ingredients:
Ice
1 ¼ cups lactose-free milk, even vegetable milk (no oat milk for
gluten-free)
1 cup Greek yogurt
1 large banana, unripe
¼ cup blueberries

Directions:
➤ Place all the necessary ingredients in a blender and blend until smooth.
➤ Serve!!!

Nutrition: Calories: 406g, Fat: 3.3g, Carbohydrates: 10.7g, Protein: 5.8g.

Basic Smoothie Base

Cooking Time: 3 Mins **Servings:1**
Ingredients:
Base
¼ tsp vanilla extract
¼ cup ice, optional
1 banana, sliced and frozen
¾ cup Greek yogurt
2 tbsp almond milk
Flavoring variations
Choconut
Pinch of salt
1 tbsp peanut butter
1 tbsp cocoa powder
Berry
½ cup strawberries, can be replaced with any other approved berry or a
mixture
5 mint leaves
Pinch of salt
Tropical
1 cup papaya, peeled and diced
1 tbsp lime juice
Pinch of salt

Directions:
➤ In a blender, blend the base ingredients and one of the flavor combinations.
➤ If ice is added, drink it right away or cover it and put it in the fridge.

Nutrition: Calories: 334g, Fat: 17g, Carbohydrates: 36g, Protein: 9g.

Sausage And Egg Omelet

Cooking Time: 8 Mins   **Servings:2**
Ingredients:
½ pound cooked, hot Easy Breakfast Sausage, cut into small pieces
¼ cup grated Cheddar cheese
¼ teaspoon sea salt
¼ teaspoon freshly ground black pepper
Nonstick cooking spray
6 eggs, beaten
¼ cup unsweetened almond milk

Directions:
➢ In a large bowl, combine the salt, eggs, almond milk, and pepper.
➢ Spray a clean skillet with cooking spray and put it over medium-high heat.
➢ Add the eggs and cook for about 3 mins until they start to solidify.
➢ With a spoon, gently pull the cooked eggs away from the edge of the pan.
➢ Tilt the skillet so any uncooked egg flows into the spaces you've created, then continue cooking the eggs for about 3 minutes more.
➢ Place the sausage and cheese over half the omelet. Fold the other side over the filling. Cook for 1 to 2 minutes more to melt the cheese.

Nutrition: Calories: 580; Fat: 36g; Carbohydrates: 2g; Protein: 60g

Breakfast Wrap

Cooking Time: 3 Mins   **Servings:1**
Ingredients:
1 tsp garlic-infused oil (optional)
½ sliced tomato
2 tbsp FODMAP-approved cheese (shredded)
1 ½ tbsp chives, chopped
1 low-FODMAP wrap
Oil for frying pan (FODMAP-approved)
2 eggs
¼ cup of spinach

Directions:
➢ Grease a frying pan with oil and place on medium heat.
➢ Mix the garlic-infused oil, eggs, and chives in a bowl before pouring into the pan. Once the mixture is almost done, carefully flip it to cook the other side.
➢ Heat the wrap according to the instructions on the packaging, and then place it onto a plate.
➢ Place the egg mixture on the wrap with enough of the wrap open so it can be rolled.
➢ Roll the wrap with the tomato, spinach, and cheese on top of the egg.

Nutrition: Calories: 247g, Fat: 17g, Carbohydrates: 9.5g, Protein 13.5g.

Sweet Green Smoothie

Cooking Time: 0 Mins   **Servings:2**
Ingredients:
1 cup freshly squeezed orange juice
1 banana
1 packet stevia (optional), plus more as needed
1 cup crushed ice
3 cups fresh baby spinach
2 cup unsweetened almond milk

Directions:
➢ In a blender, blend the orange juice, ice, spinach, almond milk, banana, and stevia (if using) until smooth, and sweeten the mixture as desired.

Nutrition: Calories:159; Fat: 4g; Carbohydrates: 30g; Protein: 4g.

Green Smoothie

Cooking Time: 0 Mins   **Servings:1**
Ingredients:
¼ cup almond milk
6 ice cubes
¼ cup Greek yogurt
1 tbsp shredded coconut
½ cup fresh pineapple, chopped and then frozen
2 tablespoons baby spinach
2 tsp chia seeds

Directions:
- Blend all the necessary ingredients in a blender except the ice and milk.
- Add the ice and blend again.
- Add the milk and continue blending until smooth.

Nutrition: Calories: 347, Fat: 24g, Carbohydrates: 31g, Protein: 8g

Carrot And Walnut Salad

Cooking Time: 5 Mins   **Servings:4**
Ingredients:
¼ cup walnuts, chopped
Pinch of salt
¼ cup orange juice
½ cup lettuce
3 carrots, peeled

Directions:
- Wash the carrots and lettuce, and then shred the lettuce in a clean bowl.
- Split the carrots into strips and combine them with the lettuce.
- Put a greased pan on a medium heat.
- Add the walnuts and fry quickly (2 minutes), stirring often to prevent the walnuts from burning.
- Remove the walnuts from the pan and place onto a paper towel. Sprinkle with salt.
- Combine the lettuce and carrots in a bowl, then add the orange juice and the walnuts before serving.

Nutrition: Calories: 277g, Fat: 2.4g, Carbohydrates: 7.5g, Protein: 1.7g.

Crunchy Granola

Cooking Time: X   **Servings: 12**
Ingredients:
2 teaspoons ground cinnamon
1/2 teaspoon sea salt
1 cup hulled sunflower seeds
1/2 cup pure maple syrup
3 tablespoons unrefined coconut oil, liquefied
4 cups gluten-free rolled oats
1/2 cup sliced almonds
2 teaspoons pure vanilla extract

Directions:
- Preheat your oven to 325°F.
- Combine all necessary ingredients in a large bowl, then place the mixture on a baking sheet lined with parchment paper.
- Cook for 50 minutes, stirring every 10–15 minutes.

Nutrition: Calories: 260, Fat: 13g, Protein: 7g, Carbohydrates: 31g.

Pineapple, Strawberry, Raspberry Smoothie

Cooking Time: 3 Mins   **Servings:2**
Ingredients:
¼ cup pineapple, fresh
1 cup almond milk, can substitute other approved milk
½ cup raspberries, frozen
1 banana, frozen and sliced
½ cup strawberries, fresh or frozen

Directions:
➢ Combine all the necessary ingredients in a large bowl.
➢ Add more milk to create a thinner consistency.

Nutrition: Calories 110g, Fat: 2.5g, Carbohydrates: 23g, Protein: 2g.

Protein Smoothie

Cooking Time: 5 Mins   **Servings:2**
Ingredients:
1 cup almond milk
1 ½ cups ice cubes
1 ½ tbsp drinking chocolate
½ banana
1 cup vanilla protein powder

Directions:
➢ Place all the necessary ingredients, except the ice, in a blender and blend.
➢ Add the ice slowly until the mixture is creamy.

Nutrition: Calories: 601g, Fat: 14.5g, Carbohydrates: 78.5g, Protein: 40.5g.

Mexican Egg Brunch

Cooking Time: X   **Servings:4**
Ingredients:
2 scallions, chopped, green part only
1/2 medium avocado, sliced into eighths
1/2 cup lactose-free sour cream
4 whole large eggs
4 egg whites
1/2 cup salsa
2 cups whole corn tortilla chips
1 cup shredded Cheddar cheese
1/2 cup sliced black olives

Directions:
➢ Preheat oven to 400°F. Grease a 9 × 13-inch glass casserole dish.
➢ Place tortilla chips in a casserole dish, then add half of the cheese.
➢ Stir eggs and egg whites until fluffy in a medium bowl, and pour eggs into the casserole dish.
➢ Pour salsa evenly over the eggs, then sprinkle on the remaining cheese. Pour on black olives and scallions.
➢ Bake for 15–20 mins or until eggs look cooked around the edges of the casserole dish.
➢ Top with avocado and sour cream.

Nutrition: Calories: 458, Fat: 23g, Protein: 20g, Carbohydrates: 46g.

Egg Wraps

Cooking Time: 5 Mins   **Servings:4**
Ingredients:
4-8 eggs
Pepper
Pinch of salt
Oil to grease the pan (from the approved food list: avocado, olive, or sunflower)

Directions:
➢ Grease a non-stick pan with oil, then place over medium heat to warm.
➢ Combine the egg in a bowl and pour it into the pan, ensuring it is spread evenly, then sprinkle with salt and pepper to taste.
➢ Cook for 30-60 secs on each side; gently flip when the edges on the first side is cooked.
➢ Place on a plate to cool, and repeat with the remaining eggs.

Nutrition: Calories: 414g, Fat: 33g, Carbohydrates: 2g, Protein: 25g.

Quiche In Ham Cups

Cooking Time: 20 Mins   **Servings:6**
Ingredients:
½ cup spring onion, green tips only
2 tbsp rice flour
Pinch of pepper
4 tbsp lactose-free milk, can be substituted with other approved milk
Pinch of salt
4 eggs, beaten
6 slices ham, cold cut, rounded
1 small bell pepper, diced

Directions:
➢ Preheat the oven to 350°F.
➢ Line 6 muffin tins with the ham slices.
➢ Combine the flour and milk, stirring constantly.

➢ Stir in the salt, eggs, and pepper, mixing until smooth, then add the spring onion and bell pepper. Pour carefully into the ham cups.
➢ Bake for 15-20 mins.
➢ It's ready when the quiche is puffy, and the ham is crispy.
➢ Allow to cool for 10 mins, then use a clean knife to lift the quiche out of the tins carefully.

Nutrition: Calories: 190g, Fat: 8.5g, Carbohydrates: 11.8g, Protein: 9.5g.

Strawberry-kiwi Smoothie with Chia Seeds

Cooking Time: x   **Servings:2**
Ingredients:
1 ripe banana, peeled and sliced
2 tablespoons maple syrup
2 tablespoons chia seeds
2 kiwifruit, peeled and sliced
¾ cup orange juice
¾ cup unsweetened rice milk
10 frozen strawberries

Directions:
➢ Place all the necessary ingredients in a blender and blend until smooth.
➢ Serve right away.

Nutrition: Calories: 294; Protein: 4g; Fat: 5g; Carbohydrates: 63g.

Quinoa Breakfast Bowl with Basil "hollandaise" Sauce

Cooking Time: 15 Mins   **Servings:4**
Ingredients:
1½ cups water
Basil "Hollandaise" Sauce (here)
½ teaspoon salt
1 cup uncooked quinoa
12 ounces green beans, trimmed and cut into 1-inch pieces

Directions:
➢ In a clean saucepan, combine the water, quinoa, green beans, and salt together, then boil over medium-high heat.
➢ Lower the heat to a low level, cover, and cook for about 15 mins until the quinoa is soft.
➢ To serve, pour the quinoa mixture into bowls and drizzle the sauce over the top.

Nutrition: Calories: 415; Protein: 9g; Fat: 28g; Carbohydrates: 36g.

Corn Salad

Cooking Time: 5 Mins   **Servings:2**
Ingredients:
1 cup cucumber
2 tbsp mayonnaise (even vegan or gluten free)
2 spring onions, green parts only
1 red capsicum
1 can (15 oz) corn
1 cup cherry tomatoes

Directions:
➢ Slice the tomatoes in half.
➢ Cut the cucumber into slices and then quarters. Chop the green part of the spring onion finely.
➢ Slice the capsicum thinly.
➢ Combine all the necessary ingredients with the mayonnaise in a bowl and serve.

Nutrition: Calories: 189g, Fat: 8g, Carbohydrates: 17g, Protein: 5g.

Easy Breakfast Sausage

Cooking Time: 8 Mins   **Servings:4**
Ingredients:
½ teaspoon sea salt
Nonstick cooking spray
⅛ teaspoon red pepper flakes
1 pound ground pork
1 teaspoon ground sage
⅛ teaspoon freshly ground black pepper

Directions:
➢ Mix the salt, red pepper flakes, pork, sage, and pepper in a large bowl.
➢ Form the mixture into eight patties.
➢ Spray a large nonstick skillet with cooking spray and place it over medium-high heat.
➢ Add the sausage patties and cook for about 4 minutes per side until browned on both sides.

Nutrition: Calories:163; Fat: 4g; Carbohydrates: <1g; Protein: 30g

CHAPTER THREE

LUNCH RECIPES

Butternut Salad with Pomegranate Seeds

Cooking Time: 20 Mins   Makes: 3 Servings
Ingredients:
¾ cups olive oil
2 tbsp. lemon juice
3-4 oz. grilled chicken breasts (optional)
½ cup feta, crumbled
½ cup loose pomegranate seeds
2-3 lb. butternut, peeled and cut into small cubes
Himalayan salt
Freshly ground black pepper
3 handfuls arugula
Directions:
➢ Set the oven to preheat at 420°F, then put the wire rack in the centre of the oven.
➢ Sprinkle the butternut cubes with salt and pepper in a large bowl, then add the oil and toss to coat.
➢ Place the butternut cubes out on a rimmed baking pan, then put it in the oven and bake for 20 minutes, tossing the cubes halfway through.
➢ The butternut should be fork-tender and slightly crisped around the edges.
➢ Set the pan aside on the counter.
➢ Toss the arugula, feta, pomegranate seeds, and lemon juice in a separate bowl, then season to taste with salt and pepper.
➢ Add the butternut and stir.
➢ If you're adding the chicken: Cut the chicken breasts into strips and add them to the salad.
➢ If you're not adding the chicken: Serve straight away.
Nutrition: Calories: 253; Protein: 5g; Fat: 15g; Carbohydrates: 27g

Bok Choy Tuna Salad

Cooking Time: 0 Mins   Makes: 2-4 Servings
Ingredients:
⅔ cups low fodmap mayonnaise
Flaky sea salt
1 tsp. Dijon mustard
5 oz. canned tuna
½ tsp. crushed tarragon
1 ½ tsp. fresh lemon juice
¾ cups bok choy stems, chopped
Freshly ground black pepper
Directions:
➢ Use a fine-mesh sieve over the sink to remove as much water from the tuna as possible. Press the water out of the tuna with a wooden spoon. Scrape the drained tuna into a large bowl.
➢ Add the mayonnaise, mustard, crushed tarragon, lemon juice, and bok choy stems and combine well.
➢ Season the mixture with flaky sea salt and black pepper. Serve
Nutrition: Calories: 112; Protein: 9g; Fat: 8g; Carbohydrates: 2g

Brown Rice & Vegetable Bowl

Cooking Time: 30 Mins   Makes: 4 Servings
Ingredients:
1 ½ tbsp. lemon juice
1 ½ tbsp. balsamic vinegar
3 tbsp. parsley, finely chopped
2 cups arugula, chopped
Freshly ground black pepper
½ tsp. brown sugar
3 tbsp. olive oil
2 cups cooked brown rice
3 cups low-FODMAP vegetables, roasted
½ cup spring onions, chopped and white parts discarded
3 tbsp. roasted pumpkin seeds
3 tbsp. feta, crumbled
Kosher salt
Directions:
➢ Roast the low-FODMAP vegetables in the oven until fork-soft and crisp around the edges, then let it cool.
➢ In a large bowl, combine the cooled roast vegetables, arugula, cooked rice, pumpkin seeds, spring onions, parsley, and feta. Sprinkle with salt and pepper. Set aside while you prepare the dressing.
➢ Combine the lemon juice, sugar, olive oil, and balsamic vinegar in a small bowl.
➢ Pour the prepared dressing over the salad and serve.
Nutrition: Calories: 146; Protein: 3g; Fat: 7g; Carbohydrates: 17g

French Salad with Mustard Dressing

Cooking Time: 15 Mins   Makes: 5 Servings
Ingredients:
1 tbsp. pure maple syrup
¼ cup brown olives, pitted
2 tomatoes, diced
8 oz. Swiss chard, chopped
4 tbsp. olive oil
1 tbsp. French mustard
4 russet potatoes, peeled and cut into wedges
Kosher salt
10 oz. green beans
1 tbsp. lemon juice
5 oz. tuna, drained
2 hard-boiled eggs, chopped

Directions:
➢ Put the potato wedges in a pot of salted water and boil for 10 mins until they are fork-soft, then drain.
➢ Blanch the green beans for 5 mins in boiling water until they brighten. Drain twice using warm water.
➢ Allow the potatoes and green beans to drain in a colander over the sink.
➢ In a small bowl, combine the French mustard, pure maple syrup, olive oil, and lemon juice until adequately combined.
➢ In a large bowl, combine the potatoes with 1 tbsp. Sauce.
➢ Place the tuna, olives, tomatoes, potatoes, green beans, Swiss chard, and chopped eggs on a serving platter. Drizzle the remaining sauce over the entire platter and serve.

Nutrition: Calories: 120; Protein: 0g; Fat: 13g; Carbohydrates: 5g

Beef & Zucchini Stir-Fry

Cooking Time: 15 Mins   Makes: 4 Servings
Ingredients:
1 lb. beef sirloin fillets, sliced across the grain
2 medium carrots, peeled and diced
1 cup zucchini, chopped
1 tbsp. oyster sauce
3 tbsp. soy sauce
8 oz. cooked low-FODMAP Asian rice noodles
1 tsp. toasted sesame oil
1 tsp. fresh ginger, grated
1 tbsp. dark brown sugar
2 tbsp. garlic-infused olive oil

Directions:
➢ Mix the dark brown sugar, oyster sauce, toasted sesame oil, ginger, and soy sauce in a small bowl. Cover the sauce while you make the remaining dish.
➢ Combine the cooked noodles with 1 tbsp garlic-infused oil in a large bowl and set aside.
➢ In a large wok over medium-high heat, heat the remaining olive oil and add in the beef strips. Stir for 4-5 minutes or until the strips are adequately cooked. Put the beef into a bowl and keep warm.
➢ Place the wok back on the stove and fry the carrots and zucchini for 3-4 mins or until fork-soft. Stir in the beef and cooked noodles before stirring in the sauce – tossing for 2-3 mins until everything is evenly coated.
➢ Serve immediately.

Nutrition: Calories: 68; Protein: 2g; Fat: 4g; Carbohydrates: 8g

Hearty Vegetarian Lettuce Bowls

Cooking Time: 0 Mins   Makes: 1 Serving
Ingredients:
½ cup brown rice
½ cup chopped walnuts
2 tsp. garlic-infused olive oil
3 pickled Jalapeños (whole)
Himalayan salt
Freshly ground black pepper
Iceberg lettuce for serving (center leaves only)

Directions:
➤ Rinse rice in water before adding it to the pot.
➤ Boil a medium pot using 3 cups of water.
➤ Add the rice and reduce the heat, but keep a steady boil. Cook, uncovered, for 30 mins. Taste the rice to check if it is done, then drain.
➤ Put the garlic-infused oil, walnuts, rice, and jalapenos into a blender and blend until you have a lumpy paste. Season to taste with salt and pepper.
➤ Pour the mixture into the lettuce bowl and serve.

Nutrition: Calories: 212; Protein: 4g; Fat: 14g; Carbohydrates: 20g

Nutty Summer Fruit Salad

Cooking Time: 0 Mins   Makes 4-6 Servings
Ingredients:
½ tsp. Himalayan salt
¾ cups toasted pecans, chopped
¼ cup fresh blueberries
¼ cup cardinal grapes, chopped
1 cup pineapple chunks 1 tbsp. poppy seeds
½ cup sunflower oil
5 tbsp. brown sugar
¼ cup red wine vinegar
½ tsp. mustard powder
2 tsp. vegan low fodmap mayonnaise
5-6 cups iceberg lettuce, chopped

½ cup fresh strawberries, sliced

Directions:
➤ Blend the sugar and red wine vinegar in a blender until most of the sugar granules have dissolved.
➤ Stir in the salt, mustard powder, and poppy seeds.
➤ With the blender running on low speed, gradually add the oil and then the mayonnaise. Scrape the sauce into a bowl and chill while you make the salad.
➤ In a large bowl, combine the fruit (blueberries, grapes, pineapple, and strawberries), lettuce, and nuts together with 4-6 tbsp. dressing.
➤ The remaining dressing can be stored in the fridge for up to 1 week using an airtight container.

Nutrition: Calories: 399; Protein: 10g; Fat: 7g; Carbohydrates: 23g

Nutty Gluten-Free Pasta Salad

Cooking Time: 20 Mins   Makes: 4 Servings
Ingredients:
1 lb. gluten-free pasta, cooked al dente
2 tbsp. sunflower oil
1 cup fresh basil, chopped
5 oz. arugula, chopped
½ cup toasted almond slivers
1 cup feta cheese, crumbled
Flaky sea salt
Freshly ground black pepper

Directions:
➤ Mix the basil, pasta, sunflower oil, and arugula in a large bowl until properly combined.
➤ Add the almonds and feta. Season to taste with salt and pepper.
➤ Serve straightaway, as this dish does not keep well.

Nutrition: Calories: 182; Protein: 3g; Fat: 6g; Carbohydrates: 34g

Nutty Chicken & Mustard Salad

Cooking Time: 0 Mins   Makes: 3-4 Servings
Ingredients:
2 tsp. lemon juice
1 tbsp. French mustard
2 tbsp. crushed tarragon
¼ cup low fodmap mayonnaise
2 cups cooked chicken, shredded
Flaky sea salt
Freshly ground black pepper
2 tbsp. lightly toasted pecans, chopped
½ cup seedless cardinal grapes

Directions:
➤ Mix the tarragon, mayonnaise, lemon juice, mustard, and chicken into a large bowl, then stir gently until everything is properly combined. Season to taste with salt and pepper.
➤ Gently add the pecans and grapes.
➤ Serve straight away, or serve as a sandwich filling on gluten-free bread.
Nutrition: Calories: 281; Protein: 32g; Fat: 9g; Carbohydrates: 21g

Blue Cheese Bacon Salad

Cooking Time: 15-20 Mins   Makes: 2-4 Servings
Ingredients:
Himalayan salt
Freshly ground black pepper
Olive oil (optional)
½ cup seedless cardinal grapes, halved
4 oz. baby spinach, chopped
2 slices thick-cut bacon, cubed
2 tbsp. spring onions, chopped (green parts only)
2 oz. blue cheese, crumbled
1 tsp. brown sugar
1 tsp. French mustard
2 tbsp. red wine vinegar

Directions:
➤ Combine the grapes, spring onions, blue cheese, and baby spinach in a bowl. Set aside while you make the remaining dish.

➤ Fry the bacon in a medium pan until the edges are crisp, then transfer the crispy bacon to a paper towel-lined plate.
➤ With the bacon fat still in the pan, add the mustard, sugar, and red wine vinegar until everything is combined perfectly. Sprinkle with salt and pepper, then add the olive oil. (You can choose not to use the olive oil)
➤ Pour the hot sauce into the bowl with the salad and top with the crispy bacon cubes. Toss and serve straight away.
Nutrition: Calories: 490; Protein: 14g; Fat: 44g; Carbohydrates: 9g

Low-FODMAP Toasted Tuna Sandwich

Cooking Time: 5 Mins   Makes: 1 Serving
Ingredients:
2 tbsp. spring onions, chopped (green parts only)
1 tbsp. parsley, chopped
¼ tsp. paprika
1 tsp. lemon juice
2 tbsp. low fodmap mayonnaise
3 oz. canned tuna in spring water, drained
Flaky sea salt
Freshly ground black pepper
2 slices gluten-free bread
2 thin slices mozzarella

Directions:
➤ Set the broiler in the oven to preheat.
➤ Mix the paprika, lemon juice, spring onions, parsley, mayonnaise, and tuna in a large bowl and season with salt and pepper.
➤ Put the available bread on a baking sheet, then divide the tuna between the two slices and spread it out evenly.
➤ Place the cheese on top of the tuna and broil in the oven until the cheese has melted.
➤ Serve immediately.

Nutrition: Calories: 443; Protein: 53g; Fat: 13g; Carbohydrates: 26g

CHAPTER FOUR

DINNER RECIPES

Wild Rice & Ginger Cod

Cooking Time: 10 Mins   Makes: 2 Servings
Ingredients:
2 tbsp. fresh ginger, peeled and grated
6 spring onions cut into strips
2 cups wild rice (cooked for serving)
2 tbsp. low-sodium soy sauce
2 skinless cod fillets
Flaky sea salt
Freshly ground black pepper
3 tbsp. clear apple cider vinegar
Directions:
➢ Thoroughly season the fish fillets with salt and pepper, then set them aside.
➢ Combine the apple cider vinegar, soy sauce, and ginger in a clean saucepan over medium-high heat.
➢ After the sauce has started to simmer, add the cod fillets and boil.
➢ When the fish is opaque and easily shreds with a fork, cover and simmer for 6 to 8 minutes. Place the spring onions on top of the salmon, then cook for three more minutes.
➢ Pour the prepared sauce over the fish and serve it right away on a bed of wild rice.
Nutrition: Calories: 300; Protein: 20g; Fat: 12g; Carbohydrates: 19g

Low-FODMAP Chicken Curry

Cooking Time: 20 Mins   Makes: 2 Servings
Ingredients:
3 large skinless chicken breasts, sliced into small cubes
Freshly ground black pepper
2 cups basmati rice, cooked for serving
2 tbsp. turmeric powder
1 tbsp. curry powder
1 tbsp. coconut oil
1 red bell pepper, diced
1 spring onion, chopped
2 tins unsweetened coconut milk
Himalayan salt
Directions:
➢ In a large frying pan over medium-high heat, melt the coconut oil before adding the bell pepper and spring onion.

➢ The vegetables should be fork-tender after frying for 3 to 5 minutes.
➢ Add the chicken cubes and stir. Fry for 7 minutes or until the chicken is fully cooked.
➢ Stir in the unsweetened coconut milk, turmeric, and curry powder. Use salt and pepper to taste to season.
➢ Place cooked basmati rice on top of the heated curry. The dish preserves well in the fridge for up to a week if it is sealed.
Nutrition: Calories: 243; Protein: 28g; Fat: 11g; Carbohydrates: 7g

Italian-Style Pasta & Shrimp

Cooking Time: 20 Mins   Makes: 6 Servings
Ingredients:
1 tsp. cayenne pepper
11 lb. large shrimp, deveined and shelled
4 cups baby spinach
8 oz. gluten-free pasta
2 tbsp. parsley, chopped
½ cup parmesan cheese, shredded
1 tbsp. lemon juice
2 tbsp. garlic-infused olive oil
6 tbsp. butter
½ tsp. crushed oregano
½ tsp. crushed thyme
½ tsp. crushed basil
Directions:
➢ Over medium-high heat, boil a pot of salted water, add the pasta, and cook. Before transferring the cooked pasta to a bowl and combining it with one tablespoon of oil, pour the spaghetti through a colander set over the sink to drain.
➢ Melt two tablespoons of butter and one tablespoon of oil in a large pot over medium-high heat. Add the shrimp after whisking the cayenne pepper into the boiling butter. The shrimp should be fried for five minutes or until they flush and their tails curl into a C. Baby spinach, oregano, thyme, and basil should be added at this point. Cook the spinach until it has roughly decreased in size to half.
➢ Fill the pot with the cooked pasta, parsley, remaining butter, and parmesan. Stir everything together thoroughly.
➢ Before serving, place the pasta on a plate and top with lemon juice.
Nutrition: Calories: 343; Protein: 25g; Fat: 8g; Carbohydrates: 37g

Mexican-Style Fish Wraps

Cooking Time: 10Mins   Makes: 4 Servings
Ingredients:
½ avocado, sliced into 8 slices
Cilantro, chopped for serving
Lime wedges for serving
1 ½ fresh limes, juiced
¼ cup taco seasoning
1 lb. halibut fillets
¼ cup low fodmap mayonnaise
1 cup red cabbage, shredded
1 cup bok choy, shredded
8 corn wraps
½ cup restaurant-style salsa
Directions:
- ➢ In a sizable bowl, mix the bok choy, mayonnaise, red cabbage, and half of the lime juice.
- ➢ Combine the remaining lime juice and taco seasoning in a different, big bowl. Place the fish fillets in the sauce, flipping after five minutes, and chill for ten minutes. Remove the sauce from the fish and place it on a platter.
- ➢ Add the oil to a sizable frying pan that has been heated to medium-high heat, then add the fish. Fry the fish for 3 to 4 mins on each side or until opaque.
- ➢ Use a microwave or a low oven to warm the wraps.
- ➢ Place the wraps on the counter and assemble them by stuffing them with equal amounts of cooked fish, covering them with salsa, and adding slices of avocado.
- ➢ Fold the tortillas, then top with cilantro. Lime wedges should be served on the side.

Nutrition: Calories: 270; Protein: 9g; Fat: 13g; Carbohydrates: 31g

Pan fried Tilapia with Olives

Cooking Time: 10Mins   Makes: 4 Servings
Ingredients:
3 tbsp. avocado oil
½ cup parsley, chopped
½ cup brown olives, pitted and halved
2 cups cherry tomatoes, halved
1 tbsp. lemon juice

4 tilapia fillets, patted dry
Flaky sea salt
Freshly ground black pepper
Directions:
- ➢ Sprinkle salt and pepper on the tilapia fillets on both sides. Place aside.
- ➢ Add the oil to a sizable frying pan that has been heated to medium-high heat before adding the fish.
- ➢ Cook the fish for 3 mins on each side or until it is opaque. The cooked fish should be placed in a dish and covered with tin foil.
- ➢ Add the parsley, olives, and tomatoes after reheating the pan. Add the lemon juice and season with a bit of salt and pepper after frying for three minutes.
- ➢ Before serving, place the fish on a plate and top with the olive sauce.

Nutrition: Calories: 186; Protein: 23g; Fat: 9g; Carbohydrates: 4g

Quick Italian Herb Chicken

Cooking Time: 25Mins   Makes: 4 Servings
Ingredients:
2 tbsp. garlic-infused olive oil
4 skinless chicken breasts
Himalayan salt
Freshly ground black pepper
3 tsp. Italian seasoning
1 cup raw quinoa
2 cups chicken stock
3 tbsp. lemon juice
Directions:
- ➢ Before adding 1 tbsp. Olive oil, heat a sizable frying pan over medium-high heat.
- ➢ Place the chicken in the hot oil after seasoning with a sprinkle of salt, some pepper, and a tablespoon of Italian seasoning. For about two minutes, sear both sides. At this stage, the chicken won't be fully cooked. While you prepare the remaining dish, set it aside on a tray.
- ➢ Reheat the pan, then add the quinoa as well as the remaining oil. Till the quinoa is thoroughly covered, toss
- ➢ Before adding the seared chicken, mix the remaining Italian seasoning, chicken stock, and lemon juice. Once the stock is cooking, cover the pot and continue to simmer until the quinoa is puffed and all the liquid has been absorbed (approx. 20 minutes).
- ➢ Plate and warmly served.

Nutrition: Calories: 292; Protein: 33g; Fat: 16g; Carbohydrates: 3g

Tangy Ground Turkey Buns

Cooking Time: 15Mins　　**Makes: 6 Servings**

Ingredients:

Sea salt

3 tbsp. soy sauce

1 tbsp. avocado oil

¼ cup light corn syrup

Freshly ground black pepper

6 gluten-free hamburger buns

½ cup low-FODMAP chicken broth

¼ cup tomato sauce

3 tbsp corn flour

1 lb. ground turkey

Directions:

➢ Heat the oil in a big skillet over medium-high heat, then add the ground turkey and cook for 3 to 5 minutes.

➢ Pour out the majority of the fat while holding back the ground turkey with a spatula.

➢ Return the skillet with the drained meat to the heat and add the corn syrup, tomato sauce, and soy sauce while stirring.

➢ In a small bowl, stir the corn flour and chicken broth while the meat and sauce are boiling. For 5-8 minutes, or until the sauce thickens, whisk the liquid into the skillet while stirring constantly. To improve taste, add salt and pepper.

➢ Put the hamburger buns on the table with the ground turkey and sauce.

Nutrition: Calories: 117; Protein: 24g; Fat: 2g; Carbohydrates: 0g

Greek-Style Lamb Skewers

Cooking Time: 6 Mins　　**Makes: 6 Servings**

Ingredients:

Avocado oil for greasing

Freshly ground black pepper

½ tsp. crushed coriander seeds

½ cup garlic-infused olive oil

½ cup plain, unsweetened lactose-free yogurt

1 red bell pepper, seeded and chopped into bite-sized pieces

2 slender zucchinis, cut into bite-sized rounds

2 lb. boneless leg of lamb, chopped into bite-sized cubes

1 green bell pepper, seeded and chopped into bite-sized pieces

1 tsp. Himalayan salt

2 tbsp. lemon juice

1 ½ tsp. ground cumin

Directions:

➢ Combine the greek yoghurt, garlic-infused olive oil, ground cumin, lemon juice, salt, and 1/2 teaspoon of black pepper in a large bowl.

➢ Before covering the bowl and chilling the food for at least 6 hours, add the lamb cubes and toss to coat.

➢ Set the oven's medium-high heat setting for the grill.

➢ To start assembling your skewers, thread the meat and vegetables in alternating directions onto the skewers.

➢ To serve as handles, leave a few inches at either end of the skewers and make sure the components are not touching. Remove any extra sauce from the bowl and discard it.

➢ Place the skewers on a baking sheet that has been lightly oiled. The skewers must not be in contact. The skewers should roast for three minutes in the oven before turning them over and cooking for a further three minutes.

Nutrition: Calories: 140; Protein: 11g; Fat: 9g; Carbohydrates: 1g

Italian-Style Beef Casserole

Cooking Time: 25Mins　　**Makes: 4 Servings**

Ingredients:

1 ½ cups chicken broth

2 tbsp. garlic-infused olive oil

Freshly ground black pepper

1 carrot, peeled and diced

6 tbsp. tomato puree

½ cup uncooked quinoa

12 oz. lean ground beef

Himalayan salt

¾ cup cold water

¼ cup red wine

1 medium red bell pepper, seeded and diced

2 tsp. low-FODMAP Italian seasoning

⅓ cups fresh basil leaves, chopped

Directions:

➢ In a pot over medium-high heat, boil the chicken stock and quinoa. For 15 to 20 mins, lower the heat and cook the quinoa. Place aside.

➢ Before adding one tablespoon of garlic-infused oil, preheat a sizable frying pan over medium-high heat. Cook the beef to the desired doneness by frying it for 7 to 10 minutes with the lid on. Add salt and pepper, along with the remaining olive oil, Italian seasoning, and chopped basil. Stir and add the carrot and bell pepper after allowing the flavours to mingle for two to three minutes.

➢ Before adding it to the pan with the other ingredients, mix the water and tomato puree together in a separate bowl. 3–4 minutes of simmering.

➢ Stir in the wine, simmer for a further five minutes, then taste and make any necessary salt and pepper adjustments.

➢ Serve the quinoa after a little stir.

Nutrition: Calories: 380; Protein: 23g; Fat: 25g; Carbohydrates: 19g

Spicy Fried Shrimp & Bok Choy

Cook Time: 5-10Mins   Makes: 6 Servings
Ingredients:
1 tsp. brown sugar
1 tsp. cayenne pepper
1 tsp. corn flour
2 tbsp. low-sodium soy sauce
½ cup chicken broth
2 tbsp. garlic-infused olive oil
2 tbsp. fresh ginger, peeled and finely chopped
3 cups bok choy
1 lb. large shrimp, peeled and deveined
2 tsp. toasted sesame oil
¼ cup spring onions, chopped (green parts only)

Directions:
- Combine the sugar, cayenne pepper, corn flour, soy sauce, and chicken broth in a medium bowl. While you make the rest of the dish, set aside.
- Fry the ginger for one minute in the oil in a big skillet over medium heat.
- Increase the heat, add the shrimp, and stir for 30-60 secs, or until the shrimp turn pink.
- After adding the bok choy and stock, stir for approximately a minute or until the sauce thickens. Add the sesame oil and spring onions after turning the heat off.
- Serve hot on a plate.

Nutrition: Calories: 376; Protein: 29g; Fat: 5g; Carbohydrates: 56g

Balsamic-glazed Salmon & Swiss Chard

Cooking Time: 15 Mins   Makes: 2 Servings
Ingredients:
2 center-cut salmon fillets
Flaky sea salt
Freshly ground black pepper
1 tsp. dark brown sugar
2 tbsp. water
3 tbsp. balsamic vinegar
1 tbsp. garlic-infused olive oil
6 oz. Swiss chard

Directions:
- Sprinkle the salmon fillets with a large amount of salt and pepper after letting them dry on paper towels. Place aside.
- Combine the sugar, water, and balsamic vinegar in a tiny glass bowl.
- While you prepare the remaining ingredients, keep two plates warm.
- Add one tablespoon of oil to a clean frying pan that has been heated to medium-high heat. Fry the fillets for 2-4 minutes on each side or until the skin is crispy but the centre is still raw. To keep the fish warm, place it on the warmed plates and tent with foil.
- Add the Swiss chard and the remaining oil to the pan, and cook for 1 to 2 minutes, or until the chard just starts to wilt and string all over (coat the chard in the oil). On the same plate as the fish, add the cooked chard and then the lid.
- For 30 seconds, whisk the glaze mixture into the hot pan until it thickens. The glaze should be applied over the fillets right away.

Nutrition: Calories: 302; Protein: 36g; Fat: 12g; Carbohydrates: 8g

CHAPTER FIVE

MEAT RECIPES

Breaded Fish Fillets with Spicy Pepper Relish

Cooking Time: 15 Mins   Servings:4
Ingredients:
2 tablespoons capers, drained and rinsed
1 jalapeño pepper, minced
Juice of 1 lime
¼ teaspoon red pepper flakes
⅛ teaspoon freshly ground black pepper
2 eggs, beaten
1 tablespoon Dijon mustard
2 cups gluten-free bread crumbs (see Tip)
1¼ teaspoons sea salt, divided
1 teaspoon dried thyme
1 pound cod, cut into 8 pieces
1 red bell pepper, chopped
Directions:
➤ Set the oven's temperature to 425°F.
➤ Combine the bread crumbs, one teaspoon of salt, pepper, and thyme in a small basin.
➤ Combine the eggs and mustard in a different small bowl.
➤ To coat the fish, dip it into the egg mixture and also the breadcrumb mixture.
➤ On a baking sheet with a nonstick rim, put the fish.
➤ Bake the fish for about 15 mins or until the fish is opaque and the crust is brown.
➤ Combine the bell pepper, capers, jalapenos, lime juice, red pepper flakes, and the remaining 1/4 teaspoon salt in a small bowl while the fish cooks.
➤ Serve the fish with the relish on top.
Nutrition: Calories: 209;   Fat: 3g; Carbohydrates: 13g; Protein: 30g

Pan-seared Scallops with Sautéed Kale

Cooking Time: 15 Mins   Servings:4
Ingredients:
⅛ teaspoon freshly ground black pepper
3 cups stemmed, chopped kale leaves
Juice of 1 orange
Zest of 1 orange
2 tablespoons extra-virgin olive oil
1 pound sea scallops
½ teaspoon sea salt
Directions:
➤ Heat the olive oil to shimmer in a sizable nonstick skillet over medium-high heat. To evenly distribute the oil, swirl the pan.
➤ Use salt and pepper to season the scallops. They should cook for around three minutes on each side in the heated skillet. The scallops should be moved to a plate and covered with foil to stay warm. Put the skillet back on the burner.
➤ Fill the skillet with the kale. While stirring, cook for about 5 minutes.
➤ Add the orange zest and juice. Cook for additional 3 mins.
➤ Place the scallops over the kale that has been sautéed.

Nutrition: Calories:199;   Fat: 8g; Carbohydrates: 11g; Protein: 21g

Garden Veggie Dip Burgers

Cooking Time: x   Servings:4
Ingredients:
1/2 cup packed baby spinach leaves, chopped
1 teaspoon sea salt
1 pound lean ground beef
2 tablespoons light sour cream
1 large carrot, peeled and diced
1/2 medium red bell pepper, seeded and diced

Directions:
➤ Blend sour cream, spinach, carrot, pepper, and salt in a blender until smooth.
➤ Combine the vegetable mixture with the ground beef in a large basin. Create four patties. Before grilling, refrigerate patties for 12 to 24 hours.
➤ Set a grill to 350°F, whether it is gas or charcoal. Grill patties for 5 minutes on each side or until internal temperature reaches 160°F.

Nutrition: Calories: 177, Fat: 7g, Protein: 25g, Carbohydrates: 3g.

Moroccan Fish Stew with Cod, Fennel, Potatoes, and Tomatoes

Cooking Time: 15 Mins   **Servings:4**

Ingredients:

1 cup water

1 pound new potatoes, halved or quartered

2 tablespoons Garlic Oil (here)

2 tablespoons chopped fresh parsley

1 teaspoon salt

½ teaspoon freshly ground black pepper

1¼ pounds cod fillets, cut into 2-inch chunks

1 teaspoon ground turmeric

1 cinnamon stick

⅛ teaspoon cayenne

1 (14½-ounce) can onion- and garlic-free diced tomatoes with juice

1 tablespoon olive oil

1 tablespoon minced fresh ginger

1 teaspoon ground cumin

1 large fennel bulb, cored and thinly sliced

Directions:

➢ In a big skillet over medium heat, warm the olive oil.

➢ Stirring constantly; add and sauté the turmeric, cinnamon stick, ginger, cumin, and cayenne for one minute.

➢ Add the potatoes, water, fennel, potatoes, salt, and pepper, along with the tomatoes and their juice. The potatoes should be soft after about 10 minutes of cooking with continuous tossing.

➢ Add the fish and heat for about 5 minutes or until the fish is well cooked. Take out and throw out the cinnamon stick.

➢ Garnish with parsley and a splash of garlic oil before serving hot.

Nutrition: Calories: 306; Protein: 28g; Fat: 6g; Carbohydrates: 33g.

Creamy Smoked Salmon Pasta

Cooking Time: 9 Mins   **Servings:4**

Ingredients:

8 ounces gluten-free pasta, cooked according to the package directions and drained

12 ounces smoked salmon, flaked

¾ cup unsweetened almond milk

2 tablespoons Garlic Oil

6 scallions, green parts only, chopped

2 tablespoons capers, drained

2 tablespoons chopped fresh dill

⅛ teaspoon freshly ground black pepper

Directions:

➢ Heat the garlic oil in a sizable nonstick skillet over moderate heat until it shimmers.

➢ Add the capers and scallions. While stirring, cook for 2 minutes.

➢ Add the salmon and cook for another two minutes.

➢ Add the pepper, dill, and almond milk and cook for 3 mins.

➢ Combine with heated pasta.

Nutrition: Calories:287;   Fat: 6g; Carbohydrates: 35g; Protein: 23g

Cumin Turkey With Fennel

Cooking Time: x   **Servings:4**

Ingredients:

1/4 teaspoon kosher salt

1 fennel bulb (about 1/2 pound), cut into 1" chunks

1 tablespoon olive oil

2 pounds lean turkey fillets

1/2 teaspoon freshly ground black pepper

1/4 teaspoon cayenne pepper

1 tablespoon brown sugar

1/4 teaspoon ground cinnamon

1/2 tablespoon ground cumin

1 cup cubed celeriac

1 cup halved seedless red grapes

Directions:

➢ Set the oven to 425°F. Place rack in oven's upper third.

➢ In a separate bowl, combine the cumin, salt, brown sugar, cinnamon, pepper, and cayenne.

➢ Mix grapes, celeriac, and fennel with oil and half of the spice mixture in a medium bowl. Spread out uniformly in a single layer on an edged baking sheet about 18" by 13".

➢ Arrange the turkey fillets on top of the grapes and vegetables and rub the remaining spice mixture on both sides.

➢ Bake for 40 minutes; after 30 minutes, check to see if the food is burning, and if it is, move the pan to a lower rack.

Nutrition: Calories: 354, Fat: 7g, Protein: 52g, Carbohydrates: 19g.

Chili-lime Shrimp And Bell Peppers

Cooking Time: 10 Mins   **Servings:4**
Ingredients:
3 tablespoons Garlic Oil
1 red bell pepper, chopped
1 pound shrimp, peeled and deveined
Juice of 1 lime
1 teaspoon chili powder
½ teaspoon sea salt
⅛ teaspoon cayenne pepper
⅛ teaspoon freshly ground black pepper

Directions:
➢ Heat the garlic oil in a sizable nonstick skillet over moderate heat until it shimmers.
➢ Add the bell pepper. While stirring, cook for 3 minutes.
➢ Add the shrimp. When it turns pink, cook for about 5 mins while stirring occasionally.
➢ Add the salt, cayenne, chili powder, lime juice, and pepper. For two minutes, cook.

**Nutrition: Calories:360;   Fat: 11g;
Carbohydrates: 38g; Protein: 28g**

Chicken And Rice With Peanut Sauce

Cooking Time: 10 Mins   **Servings:4**
Ingredients:
½ cup sugar-free natural peanut butter
Juice of 1 lime
2 cups cooked brown rice
½ cup coconut milk
2 tablespoons gluten-free soy sauce
2 tablespoons Garlic Oil
1 pound boneless skinless chicken thigh meat, cut into strips
1 tablespoon peeled and grated fresh ginger

Directions:
➢ Heat the garlic oil in a sizable nonstick skillet over moderate heat until it shimmers.
➢ Add the chicken and simmer, stirring frequently, for about 6 mins or until browned.

➢ Combine the coconut milk, soy sauce, ginger, peanut butter, and lime juice in a small bowl. Include it with the chicken.
➢ Stir in rice. Cook for additional 3 mins while stirring.

**Nutrition: Calories:718;   Fat: 40g;
Carbohydrates: 46g, Protein: 46g**

Pork And Fennel Meatballs

Cooking Time: x   **Servings:24**
Ingredients:
1/4 teaspoon salt
1/2 teaspoon freshly ground black pepper
11/2 tablespoons olive oil
2 teaspoons fennel seeds
3 tablespoons gluten-free panko bread crumbs
1 large egg
1/8 teaspoon wheat-free asafetida powder
1 pound lean ground pork
2 tablespoons roughly chopped fresh flat-leaf parsley

Directions:
➢ Combine the pork, parsley, bread crumbs, egg, asafetida, salt, and pepper in a mixing dish. Stir or thoroughly blend with your hands. Form the meat into 1-inch balls.
➢ Toast fennel seeds in oil for about 4 minutes, or until they are aromatic, in a medium skillet over medium heat. Place the meatballs in the pan.
➢ Cook meatballs for 20 minutes total, browning them on all sides for 4-5 minutes. Meatballs are fully cooked when the insides are no longer pink.

Nutrition: Calories: 64, Fat: 5g, Protein: 4g, Carbohydrates: 1g.

Sautéed Shrimp With Cilantro-lime Rice

Cooking Time: 10 Mins   **Servings:4**
Ingredients:
¼ cup Cilantro-Lime Vinaigrette
½ teaspoon sea salt
3 tablespoons Garlic Oil
1 pound medium shrimp, peeled and deveined
2 cups cooked brown rice

Directions:
- ➢ Heat the garlic oil in a sizable nonstick skillet over moderate heat until it shimmers.
- ➢ Add the shrimp next. When the shrimp are pink, cook for about 5 minutes, stirring regularly.
- ➢ Add the vinaigrette, salt, and rice. Cook for a further 2 minutes while stirring.

Nutrition: Calories: 360; Fat: 11g Carbohydrates: 38g, Protein: 28g

Dijon-roasted Pork Tenderloin

Cooking Time: 60 Mins   **Servings:8**
Ingredients:
¼ cup brown sugar
½ teaspoon pepper
¼ cup whole-grain Dijon mustard
1 pork loin roast (about 4 pounds), trimmed of excess fat
1 teaspoon salt
Directions:
- ➢ Set the oven's temperature to 425°F.
- ➢ Sprinkle the roast with salt and pepper all over, set it on a roasting rack in a roasting pan, and cook it for 30 minutes in the preheated oven.
- ➢ After applying mustard to the entire roast, sprinkle brown sugar on top and mix it in with the mustard.
- ➢ Reduce the oven's temperature to 375°F and roast the meat for an additional 30 minutes, basting frequently with the pan drippings, or until a meat thermometer inserted into the middle of the roast registers 145°F. The roast should be taken out of the oven, covered

loosely with foil, and rested for 10 minutes before slicing.
- ➢ To assemble the dish, cut the roast into 1-inch-thick slices and top each with a small amount of the pan drippings.

Nutrition: Calories: 499; Protein: 65g; Fat: 22g; Carbohydrates: 5g.

Beef Stir-fry with Chinese Broccoli And Green Beans

Cooking Time: x   **Servings:4**
Ingredients:
1 tablespoon gluten-free, onion-free, garlic-free oyster sauce
¼ teaspoon cayenne pepper
¼ cup (60 ml) sesame oil
1 pound (450 g) beef sirloin or top round steak, very thinly sliced
1 bunch Chinese broccoli, cut into 1-inch (3 cm) lengths
1 heaping tablespoon grated ginger
2 teaspoons garlic-infused olive oil
2 teaspoons olive oil
7 ounces (200 g) green beans, trimmed (1¾ cups)
1 cup (80 g) bean sprouts
Steamed rice or prepared rice noodles, for serving
Directions:
- ➢ In a dish, mix the olive oil, two tablespoons of sesame oil, garlic-infused oil, and ginger. Add the steak and coat with the sauce. Cover and chill for two to three hours.
- ➢ In a wok over medium-high heat, warm the two tablespoons of sesame oil that are left. After adding, sauté the beef for 2 minutes or until just lightly browned. Stir-fry the Chinese broccoli, green beans, and bean sprouts for 2 to 4 minutes.
- ➢ Stir-fry the beef and veggies for 1 to 2 minutes or until the sauce is heated through. Add the oyster sauce and cayenne pepper.
- ➢ Pour rice or rice noodles on top and serve.

Nutrition: calories: 437; protein: 24g; Fat: 34g; carbohydrates: 7g.

CHAPTER SIX

FISH AND SEAFOOD RECIPES

Grilled Halibut with Lemony Pesto

Cooking Time: x   **Servings:4**

Ingredients:

4 (6-ounce) raw halibut steaks
1/2 cup Garden Pesto (see recipe in chapter 10)
1 tablespoon grapeseed oil
2 tablespoons freshly squeezed lemon juice, divided
2 teaspoons grated lemon zest, divided
1/2 teaspoon sea salt
1/4 teaspoon freshly ground black pepper

Directions:

➢ In a big bowl, combine oil, one tablespoon of lemon juice, one teaspoon of zest, salt, and pepper. Marinade the halibut for 30 minutes.
➢ Fill a blender with the pesto, remaining juice, and remaining zest and blend.
➢ Preheat a broiler, gas grill, or charcoal grill to 350°F. For about 6 minutes on each side, grill or broil steaks until done.
➢ Add the lemony pesto on top of the fish and serve right away.

Nutrition: Calories: 356, Fat: 20g, Protein: 39g, Carbohydrates: 3g

Rita's Linguine with Clam Sauce

Cooking Time: x   **Servings:4**

Ingredients:

1/8 teaspoon wheat-free asafetida powder
1/4 cup coarsely chopped fresh flat-leaf parsley
1/2 teaspoon freshly ground black pepper
2 tablespoons unsalted butter, divided
1/2 cup dry white wine
1 teaspoon dried oregano
12 ounces gluten-free linguine
1 tablespoon olive oil
1 tablespoon garlic-infused olive oil
2 dozen cherrystone clams, rinsed and scrubbed

Directions:

➢ Prepare pasta as directed on the package until al dente. After draining the pasta, save 1/2 cup of the water. Place aside.
➢ In a 5-quart saucepan, heat the oils over medium heat as the pasta cooks.
➢ Add one tablespoon of butter, wine, asafetida, and oregano, then heat for 2 minutes.
➢ Add the clams; cover the pot and boil for 10 minutes or until the clams open. Discard any clams that have not opened.
➢ Stir pasta and clams for one minute.
➢ Add black pepper, one tablespoon of butter, parsley, and any remaining pasta water after removing from the stove. Serve right away.

Nutrition: Calories: 456, Fat: 14g, Protein: 12g, Carbohydrates: 65g.

Shrimp Puttanesca with Linguine

Cooking Time: x   **Servings:4**

Ingredients:

1 pound gluten-free linguine
2 tablespoons olive oil
1 (24-ounce) can diced tomatoes
2 cups shredded kale
1/2 cup black olives
1/2 cup green olives
2 tablespoons capers, rinsed and drained
1 teaspoon red pepper flakes
1 pound large shrimp
1/2 cup crumbled feta cheese

Directions:

➢ Prepare pasta as directed on the package. Drain, then set apart.
➢ In a big skillet, heat the oil over medium heat. Add the tomatoes, greens, capers, red pepper flakes, black and green olives, and olives. After bringing it to a boil, lower the heat to a simmer, and cook for 15 minutes.
➢ Add cheese, pasta, and shrimp to the sauce. Cook the shrimp for 3–5 mins or until done.

Nutrition: Calories: 529, Fat: 18g, Protein: 42g, Carbohydrates: 98g.

Cedar Planked Salmon

Cooking Time: x **Servings:4**
Ingredients:
1/4 teaspoon sea salt
1/8 teaspoon pure vanilla extract
12-ounce raw salmon fillet
Cedar grilling plank
1 tablespoon demerara sugar
1 teaspoon freshly ground tricolored peppercorns

Directions:
➢ Soak the cedar board in warm water for at least 60 mins.
➢ Combine salt, sugar, peppercorns, and vanilla in a small bowl. Place salmon on the prepared plank with the skin side down and rub all over.
➢ Preheat a broiler, gas grill, or charcoal grill to 350°F. Salmon on a board should be grilled or broiler-cooked for 15 minutes.

Nutrition: Calories: 133, Fat: 5g, Protein: 17g, Carbohydrates: 4g.

Atlantic Cod With Basil Walnut Sauce

Cooking Time: x **Servings:4**
Ingredients:
Zest of 1 large lemon
3 tablespoons extra-virgin olive oil, divided
1/4 packed cup fresh basil leaves
2 (6-ounce) Atlantic cod fillets
1/4 teaspoon kosher salt, divided
1/2 teaspoon freshly ground black pepper, divided
1 tablespoon small walnut pieces

Directions:
➢ Set the oven to 400°F.
➢ Arrange the fish fillets in a 9 x 13 baking dish and season both sides with 18

teaspoon salt, 14 teaspoon pepper, and lemon zest. Use one tablespoon of olive oil to brush the fish.
➢ Blend basil, walnuts, 1/8 teaspoon salt, and 1/4 teaspoon pepper in a food processor. Process until paste forms. Add two tablespoons of olive oil gradually while the machine is running. Over the fish, evenly pat the mixture.
➢ Bake the dish in the oven for 13–17 minutes or until the flesh is completely opaque in color.
➢ Serve the fish and rice together, along with the pan juices.
Nutrition: Calories: 176, Fat: 12g, Protein: 16g, Carbohydrates: 2g.

Coconut Shrimp

Cooking Time: x **Servings:4**
Ingredients:
1 slice gluten-free bread, toasted
1/2 cup unsweetened finely shredded coconut
1/8 teaspoon sea salt
1 large egg
1/8 teaspoon pure vanilla extract
16 large raw shrimp, peeled and deveined

Directions:
➢ Set the oven to 425°F. Spray coconut oil on a baking pan after lining it with foil.
➢ Place the toast in the blender. Blend until fragments of bread become fine.
➢ Combine salt, coconut, and bread crumbs in a flat dish.
➢ Whisk the egg and vanilla in a separate dish.
➢ Coat each shrimp with bread crumbs and coconut mixture after dipping it in egg mixture. Place on a baking sheet.
➢ Five minutes of baking. Bake for a further five mins, or until the shrimp are completely cooked through, after carefully turning each one over. Serve right away.

Nutrition: Calories: 88, Fat: 5g, Protein: 5g, Carbohydrates: 6g.

Cornmeal-crusted Tilapia

Cooking Time: x   **Servings:2**
Ingredients:
1/2 teaspoon salt
1 tablespoon lactose-free milk
1 tablespoon sunflower oil
1 teaspoon freshly ground black pepper
1/8 teaspoon wheat-free asafetida powder
1 pound tilapia
1/4 cup gluten-free bread crumbs
3/4 cup coarse cornmeal
2 tablespoons gluten-free all-purpose flour
1 large egg
Directions:
➢ Rinse and dry the fish. Cut into two pieces.
➢ Mix the bread crumbs, cornmeal, flour, salt, pepper, and asafetida in a big basin. Egg and milk should be combined in a small bowl.
➢ Dip the tilapia in the egg mixture and shake off any extra, then coat the fish on both sides with the cornmeal mixture.
➢ In a 9" frying pan, heat the oil over medium-high heat. Cook fish in a pan for 3 to 5 minutes on each side until opaque and flaky.

Nutrition: Calories: 561, Fat: 13g, Protein: 50g, Carbohydrates: 58g.

Shrimp And Cheese Casserole

Cooking Time: x   **Servings:4**
Ingredients:
1/8 teaspoon wheat-free asafetida powder
1/4 cup dry white wine
1/4 pound crumbled feta cheese
1/4 pound shredded mozzarella cheese
10 ounces fresh spinach, chopped
3 tablespoons butter
1/8 teaspoon salt
1/8 teaspoon freshly ground black pepper
1 (14.5-ounce) can diced tomatoes, drained
10 ounces medium shrimp, peeled and deveined
2 tablespoons olive oil
Directions:
➢ Set the oven to 350°F. Make a 9" x 13" casserole dish greased.
➢ Melt the butter in a clean skillet over moderate heat. Stir in the asafetida, salt, and pepper.
➢ Cook the spinach and wine for two to three minutes.
➢ Add diced tomatoes on top of the spinach mixture in the casserole dish that has been prepared. Olive oil should be drizzled over the shrimp. Add some feta and mozzarella.
➢ Bake for 25 minutes, or until cheese bubbles and starts to turn golden.
Nutrition: Calories: 346, Fat: 22g, Protein: 27g, Carbohydrates: 8g.

Baked Moroccan-style Halibut

Cooking Time: x   **Servings:4**
Ingredients:
4 (6-ounce) fresh halibut fillets
2 tablespoons olive oil
1/2 teaspoon ground cumin
1/4 teaspoon ground cinnamon
1/4 teaspoon freshly ground black pepper
1 pint cherry tomatoes
1/4 cup pitted black olives
1/8 teaspoon wheat-free asafetida powder
Directions:
➢ Set the oven to 450°F.
➢ Combine the asafetida, cumin, cinnamon, tomatoes, olives, and black pepper in a medium mixing bowl.
➢ Place the halibut in a big baking pan. Distribute the tomato mixture over the fish evenly. Put some oil on the fish.
➢ Bake for 10 to 15 mins or until a thermometer with an instant-read probe placed into the thickest fillet reaches 145°F. Serve right away.
Nutrition: Calories: 269, Fat: 12g, Protein: 36g, Carbohydrates: 4g.

Salmon With Herbs

Cooking Time: x   **Servings:2**
Ingredients:
1 pound salmon fillets
1/4 teaspoon salt
1/2 teaspoon freshly ground black pepper
1/4 cup plus 2 tablespoons olive oil
1/4 cup chopped fresh dill
2 tablespoons roughly chopped fresh rosemary
1/4 cup fresh flat-leaf parsley leaves
2 tablespoons fresh thyme leaves
2 tablespoons lemon juice
Directions:
➢ Set the oven to 250 ºF.
➢ Spray cooking spray on a 9" x 13" casserole dish. Put salt and pepper on the salmon skin-side down.
➢ In a food processor, combine 1/4 cup plus two tspns of olive oil with the parsley, thyme, dill, rosemary, and lemon juice. The herb paste should be applied to the fish with a spatula or your hands.
➢ Depending on the thickness of the fish, bake for 22–28 minutes. The thickest portion of the fillet should be carefully pulled with the fork's tines. Fish is cooked when it flakes readily.
➢ Place the fish on a cutting board after sliding a spatula beneath it. Slice into equal portions, then serve.
Nutrition: Calories: 588, Fat: 44g, Protein: 45g, Carbohydrates: 3g.

Glazed Salmon

Cooking Time: x   **Servings:4**
Ingredients:
1/4 cup gluten-free tamari
1 tablespoon almond butter
1 tablespoon pure maple syrup
2 teaspoons rice vinegar
2 teaspoons sesame oil
1 teaspoon blackstrap molasses
1/8 teaspoon ground ginger
12-ounce fillet of salmon
Directions:
➢ To make the glaze, combine all the ingredients in a small pot except the salmon.
➢ Pour two teaspoons of glaze into a small bowl.

➢ Preheat a broiler, charcoal barbecue, or gas grill to 350°F. With the salmon skin-side down and basted with the sauce from the small bowl, grill or broil for 15 mins.
➢ To thicken the leftover glaze, heat it over moderate heat for about 5 minutes while the salmon cooks.
➢ Remove from fire when salmon is thoroughly cooked, drizzle with warm glaze, and serve.
Nutrition: Calories: 190, Fat: 10g, Protein: 19g, Carbohydrates: 6g.

Coconut-crusted Fish with Pineapple Relish

Cooking Time: x   **Servings:2**
Ingredients:
1/2 cup shredded unsweetened coconut
1/2 cup gluten-free panko bread crumbs
1/2 teaspoon paprika
1 large egg
1 pound cod fillets
2 cups chopped pineapple
1/4 cup finely chopped red bell pepper
1 tablespoon fresh lemon juice
2 teaspoons palm sugar
1 finely chopped seeded jalapeño pepper
1/8 teaspoon salt

Directions:
➢ Set the oven to 400°F.
➢ Combine the coconut, bread crumbs, and paprika in a medium basin.
➢ Whisk the egg in a separate, tiny bowl. Fish fillets should be coated with egg, then coconut-panko mixture.
➢ Put the dish in a baking pan and bake for 12 to 15 minutes, or until it is firm.
➢ To make pineapple relish, mix sugar, lemon juice, pineapple, bell pepper, and jalapenos; whisk in salt. Serve the fish with the relish on top.
Nutrition: Calories: 423, Fat: 11g, Protein: 46g, Carbohydrates: 36g.

Grilled Cod with Fresh Basil

Cooking Time: x   **Servings:4**
Ingredients:
8 tablespoons butter (1 stick)
2 pounds cod fillet
2 tablespoons chopped fresh basil
1 garlic clove, peeled, slightly smashed
1 pinch ground red pepper
3 tablespoons extra-virgin olive oil
Juice of 1 medium lemon
Directions:
➢ In a small dish, mix the oil and lemon juice. Cod is added, and it is coated. Marinate for 30 mins at room temperature.
➢ Heat a gas grill or even charcoal to 350ºF. Grill fish for 15 minutes, turning once after 8 minutes or until cooked through.
➢ When the fish is on the second side, combine the butter and garlic in a small saucepan and heat for 5 minutes. Remove and discard the garlic, then turn the heat off and stir in the basil and red pepper flakes.
➢ Take the cod off the grill, and serve it with a side of basil sauce.
Nutrition: Calories: 400, Fat: 25g, Protein: 40g, Carbohydrates: 1g.

Grilled Swordfish With Pineapple Salsa

Cooking Time: x   **Servings:4**
Ingredients:
4 (3.5-ounce) swordfish steaks, 1" thick
2 tablespoons olive oil
1/2 whole pineapple, cut into small chunks
1/4 teaspoon kosher salt
2 tablespoons finely chopped cilantro
2 medium limes, juiced and zested
1 medium orange, juiced and zested
1/2 teaspoon freshly ground black pepper
Directions:

➢ Mix lime, pineapple, cilantro, orange juice, and zest in a medium bowl; put aside.
➢ Preheat a cast-iron skillet over moderate heat or a medium-high setting on a gas grill. Put salt and pepper in a small bowl and combine.
➢ Oil-brush the swordfish and season with salt and pepper.
➢ When cooking fish, cook it for 5 minutes on one side and 3 minutes on the other.
➢ Place the swordfish on plates and add the pineapple salsa on top.

Nutrition: Calories: 267, Fat: 11g, Protein: 20g, Carbohydrates: 24g.

Basic Baked Scallops

Cooking Time: x   **Servings:2**
Ingredients:
1/2 teaspoon smoked paprika
2 tablespoons olive oil
1/4 teaspoon sea salt
1/2 teaspoon freshly ground black pepper
2 tablespoons chopped fresh flat-leaf parsley
3/4 pound sea scallops
2 tablespoons lemon juice
21/2 tablespoons unsalted butter, melted
1/2 cup gluten-free bread crumbs

Directions:
➢ Set the oven to 425 ºF.
➢ In a 2-quart baking dish, combine the lemon juice, salt, scallops, melted butter, and pepper.
➢ Mix the paprika, parsley, bread crumbs, and olive oil in a medium bowl. Sprinkle over the scallops.
➢ Bake for 12 to 14 mins, or until bread crumbs are brown and scallops are heated through. Serve right away.

Nutrition: Calories: 426, Fat: 30g, Protein: 17g, Carbohydrates: 23g.

CHAPTER SEVEN

VEGETARIAN RECIPES

Spanish Rice

Cooking Time: 10 Mins   Servings:4
Ingredients:
1 cup canned crushed tomatoes, drained
½ teaspoon sea salt
¼ teaspoon freshly ground black pepper
½ cup Low-FODMAP Vegetable Broth
½ cup chopped black olives
2 tablespoons Garlic Oil
6 scallions, green parts only, chopped
2 cups hot cooked brown rice
½ cup pine nuts
1 teaspoon dried oregano

Directions:
➤ Heat the garlic oil in a big skillet over moderate heat until it shimmers.
➤ Add the scallions next. With occasional stirring, cook for 3 minutes.
➤ Add the oregano, brown rice, broth, olives, pine nuts, tomatoes, salt, and pepper. Cook, stirring, for another 5 mins or more or until well heated.

Nutrition: Calories: 399; Fat: 22g;
Carbohydrates: 46g; Protein: 8g

Pasta With Pesto Sauce

Cooking Time: 0 Mins   Servings:4
Ingredients:
8 ounces gluten-free angel hair pasta, cooked according to the package
instructions. Drained
1 recipe Macadamia Spinach Pesto
¼ cup grated Parmesan cheese

Directions:
➤ Combine the noodles and pesto in the warm saucepan you used to cook the pasta.
➤ Add a cheese garnish.

Pineapple Fried Rice

Cooking Time: 10 Mins   Servings:4
Ingredients:
2 tablespoons gluten-free soy sauce
¼ cup chopped fresh cilantro leaves
1 tablespoon peeled and grated fresh ginger
3 cups cooked brown rice
2 cups canned pineapple (in juice), drained, ¼ cup juice reserved
2 tablespoons Garlic Oil
6 scallions, green parts only, finely chopped
½ cup canned water chestnuts, drained

Directions:
➤ Heat the garlic oil in a big skillet over moderate heat until it shimmers.
➤ Add the scallions, ginger, and water chestnuts. While stirring, cook for 5 minutes.
➤ Add the pineapple, brown rice, and soy sauce. Reserve the juice from the pineapple. Rice should be heated through after 5 minutes of stirring.
➤ Add the cilantro and stir.

Nutrition: Calories: 413; Fat: 9g;
Carbohydrates: 77g; Protein: 7g

Stuffed Zucchini Boats

Cooking Time: 40 Mins   Servings:4
Ingredients:
2 cups cooked brown rice
½ teaspoon sea salt
⅛ teaspoon freshly ground black pepper
½ cup canned crushed tomatoes, drained
4 medium zucchini, halved lengthwise with the middles scooped out, chopped, and reserved
½ cup grated Parmesan cheese
¼ cup chopped fresh basil leaves

Directions:
➢ Turn on the oven to 400°F.
➢ Lay the zucchini halves, cut-side up, on a baking sheet with a rim.
➢ Combine the basil, Parmesan cheese, brown rice, tomatoes, saved diced zucchini, salt, and pepper in a medium bowl. Fill the zucchini boats with the mixture by spoon.
➢ Bake the zucchini for 40 to 45 mins, or until they are tender.

Nutrition: Calories: 262; Fat: 5g; Carbohydrates: 46g; Protein: 11g

Turmeric Rice with Cranberries

Cooking Time: x   Servings:2
Ingredients:
1/4 teaspoon sea salt
1 cup cooked basmati rice
1/2 cup no-sugar-added dried cranberries
2 cups lukewarm water
1/16 teaspoon wheat-free asafetida powder
1/2 teaspoon saffron dissolved in 1/4 cup hot water
2 tablespoons light brown sugar
1 tablespoon coconut oil
2 tablespoons pine nuts
1/2 teaspoon ground turmeric

Directions:
➢ To make cranberries plumper, soak them in lukewarm water for about 10 minutes, then drain.
➢ Heat coconut oil in a wok or medium skillet over moderate heat. Add cranberries and pine nuts.
➢ Lower heat to low and stir in the saffron, sugar, turmeric, asafetida, and salt. Cook for 7 minutes.
➢ Add the rice and toss until it is thoroughly coated.
Nutrition: Calories: 396, Fat: 16g, Protein: 4g, Carbohydrates: 63g.

Peanut Butter Soba Noodles

Cooking Time: 0 Mins   Servings:4
Ingredients:
1 packet stevia
8 ounces soba noodles, cooked according to the package directions, drained, and hot
6 tablespoons sugar-free natural peanut butter
¼ cup low-sodium gluten-free soy sauce
1 tablespoon Garlic Oil
1 teaspoon peeled and grated fresh ginger
2 tablespoons freshly squeezed lime juice

Directions:
➢ Combine the lime juice, garlic oil, ginger, peanut butter, soy sauce, and stevia in a small bowl or blender and blend until smooth.
➢ Mix the hot noodles and sauce in a large serving bowl and toss to coat.

Nutrition: Calories: 357; Fat: 13g; Carbohydrates: 49g; Protein: 17g

Vegetable Stir-fry

Cooking Time: 10 Mins   Servings:4
Ingredients:
2 cups broccoli florets
½ cup Stir-Fry Sauce
2 tablespoons Garlic Oil
2⅔ cups chopped firm tofu
8 scallions, green parts only, chopped

Directions:
➤ Heat the garlic oil in a big skillet over moderate heat until it shimmers.
➤ Add the scallions, broccoli, and tofu. Broccoli should be crisp-tender after cooking for around 7 minutes while tossing often.
➤ Add the stir-fry sauce and mix. As it thickens, cook for about 3 mins while stirring.

Nutrition: Calories: 231; Fat: 14g; Carbohydrates: 14g; Protein: 16g

Cheese Strata

Cooking Time: 30 Mins   Servings:4
Ingredients:
½ teaspoon sea salt
¾ cup grated Monterey Jack cheese
⅛ teaspoon freshly ground black pepper
Nonstick cooking spray
3 eggs, beaten
1 cup unsweetened almond milk
5 slices gluten-free sandwich bread, crusts removed, cut into cubes

Directions:
➤ Set the oven's heat to 350°F.
➤ Coat a loaf pan measuring 9 by 5 inches with nonstick cooking spray.
➤ Combine the almond milk, salt, eggs, and pepper in a medium bowl.
➤ After mixing the bread, thoroughly coat it in the egg mixture.

➤ Add the cheese.
➤ Place the prepared dish in the oven and bake for 30 to 35 mins, or until the filling is set.

Nutrition: Calories: 402; Fat: 29g; Carbohydrates: 28g; Protein: 12g

Vegetable Nori Roll

Cooking Time: x   Servings:1
Ingredients:
1 small cucumber, peeled and cut into thin slices
1/8 medium avocado, thinly sliced
Pulp of 1 small lemon slice, cut into thirds
1 perforated half cut (0.08-ounce) nori sheet
1/2 tablespoon tahini
1 ounce medium tofu, drained, patted dry
1/8 cup peeled and shredded carrot

Directions:
➤ Use a bamboo mat to arrange the nori sheet horizontally in front of you, rough side facing up.
➤ Cover the entire nori sheet with a line of tahini.
➤ Arrange the tofu, lemon, avocado, carrots, and cucumber across the bottom center of the nori sheet.
➤ Gently but firmly fold the ingredients into a sushi-like roll.
➤ Carefully cut your roll into serving pieces with a sharp knife.

Nutrition: Calories: 153, Fat: 9g, Protein: 6g, Carbohydrates: 17g.

Mixed Grains, Seeds, And Vegetable Bowl

Cooking Time: x   **Servings:4**
Ingredients:
11/2 tablespoons balsamic vinegar
1/2 teaspoon dried rosemary
1/2 cup brown rice, cooked
3/4 cup red quinoa, rinsed and cooked
3 cups baby spinach
1 cup buckwheat, rinsed and cooked
1/2 tablespoon coconut oil
1/2 teaspoon dried thyme
2 medium sweet potatoes, peeled and cut into 2" chunks
2 tablespoons olive oil
1/2 teaspoon dried oregano
2 tablespoons pumpkin seeds
11/3 of a whole fennel bulb, halved lengthwise and cut into quarters

Directions:
➤ Set the oven to 375 ºF.
➤ Sweet potatoes should be put in a medium basin. Add oregano, rosemary, oil, vinegar, and thyme. Toss to coat with your hands.
➤ Place on the rimmed baking sheet, roast for one hour, flipping halfway through, and top with fennel and pumpkin seeds.
➤ Use the same bowl you used for the sweet potatoes and add the rice, quinoa, and buckwheat. Add coconut oil and mix.
➤ As soon as the sweet potatoes are done baking and are tender, add them to the bowl. Toss in the spinach. Serve right away.
Nutrition: Calories: 411, Fat: 14g, Protein: 12g, Carbohydrates: 63g.

Eggplant And Chickpea Curry

Cooking Time: 15 Mins   **Servings:4**
Ingredients:
1 cup canned chickpeas, drained
1 cup unsweetened almond milk
1 tablespoon curry powder
¼ teaspoon freshly ground black pepper
6 scallions, green parts only, minced
2 cups chopped eggplant
2 tablespoons Garlic Oil
Directions:
➤ Heat the garlic oil in a big skillet over moderate heat until it shimmers.
➤ Add the eggplant and scallions. Cook the eggplant softly for about 5 minutes while stirring frequently.
➤ Add the almond milk, curry powder, pepper, and chickpeas, then boil. Medium-low heat should be used to simmer for 10 minutes.
Nutrition: Calories:275; Fat: 11g; Carbohydrates: 36g; Protein: 11g

Zucchini Pizza Bites

Cooking Time: 15 Mins   **Servings:4**
Ingredients:
2 tablespoons Garlic Oil
1 cup grated mozzarella cheese
2 teaspoons dried Italian seasoning
½ teaspoon sea salt
2 medium zucchini, cut into ¼-inch-thick slices
1 cup tomato sauce
Directions:
➤ Set the oven's heat to 350°F.
➤ Place parchment paper on two rimmed baking sheets. On the prepared baking pans, arrange the zucchini slices in a single layer.
➤ Combine the garlic oil, Italian seasoning, tomato sauce, and salt in a small bowl. On the sliced zucchini, spread the sauce.
➤ Add some cheese on top.
➤ Bake for approximately 15 mins or until the cheese is heated and the zucchini is soft.
Nutrition: Calories:124; Fat: 6g; Carbohydrates: 9g; Protein: 10g

CHAPTER EIGHT

SNACKS AND
DESSERTS

Fluffy Pancakes

Cooking Time: 15 Mins **Servings:16**
Ingredients:
2 tbsp white sugar
¾ cup lactose-free or coconut milk
1 egg
Batter
½ cup regular fat cream, whipped
8 tbsp strawberry jam
1 ¼ cups gluten-free flour
3 tsp baking powder
¾ tsp vanilla extract
2 tsp butter
Directions:
➢ In a bowl, stir the dry ingredients, and in the center, make a well.
➢ Add the vanilla extract, milk, and egg. Mix thoroughly until almost no lumps remain.
➢ Examine the batter. Lifting the whisk from the bowl is how you do this. If it is too thick, add a tablespoon of milk; otherwise, it should drip thickly back into the bowl.
➢ In a nonstick pan, melt the butter over medium heat. To get rid of any extra butter, wipe the pan with a paper towel.
➢ Pour two tablespoons of batter into the pan for each pancake. Pancakes should be gently flipped over when bubbles start to develop on their tops and cooked until golden on the other side. Serve warm.
Nutrition: Calories: 116, Fat: 3.8g, Carbohydrates: 18.7g, Protein: 1.4g.

Chocolate Peanut Butter Energy Bites

Cooking Time: 2 Mins **Servings:10**
Ingredients:
¼ cup peanuts, roasted, chopped
¼ cup dark chocolate, 55%, finely chopped
Pinch of salt
½ cup smooth peanut butter
1 cup oats
⅓ cup maple syrup
Directions:
➢ Combine the ingredients in a bowl.

➢ After combining, form balls out of the mixture (approximately one tablespoon in size; add more if there is mixture left once ten balls have been rolled).
➢ As they are rolled, they will need to be compressed. Use an airtight container for storage.

Nutrition: Calories: 240, Fat: 11g, Carbohydrates: 29g, Protein: 8g

Spiced Tortilla Chips

Cooking Time: 15 Mins **Servings:4**
Ingredients:
12 (6-inch) corn tortillas
1 tablespoon vegetable oil
1 teaspoon ground cumin
1 teaspoon gluten-free, onion- and garlic-free chili powder
1 teaspoon salt

Directions:
➢ Set the oven's heat to 350°F.
➢ Make eight wedges out of each tortilla. On a sizable baking sheet, put the wedges in a single layer and brush the wedges with oil on both sides.
➢ Combine the salt, cumin, and chili powder in a small bowl. Evenly distribute the spice mixture over the chips.
➢ For around 7 minutes, bake the chips. Bake the chips for a further 7 to 8 minutes on the other side or until they are crisp and golden brown. Either serve hot or let cool to room temperature.
➢ For up to three days, cooled chips can be kept on the counter in a sealed container.

Nutrition: Calories: 189; Protein: 4g; Fat: 6g; Carbohydrates: 32g.

Low-fodmap Hummus

Cooking Time: 0 Mins   **Servings:4**
Ingredients:
Juice of 1 lemon
½ teaspoon sea salt
1 zucchini
2 tablespoons tahini
2 tablespoons Garlic Oil
Assorted low-FODMAP veggies, for dipping

Directions:
- ➢ Blend the zucchini, tahini, garlic oil, lemon juice, and salt in a blender. until smooth, process.
- ➢ Serve the vegetables with the dip.

Nutrition: Calories:116; Fat: 11g;
Carbohydrates: 4g; Protein: 2g.

Lemon Bar

Cooking Time: 50 Mins   **Servings:16**
Ingredients:
2 tbsp water
Lemon
4 eggs, large
½ cup lemon juice
Crust
1 ½ cups gluten-free flour
½ cup white sugar
½ cup butter, unsalted
1 ½ cups sugar
¼ cup gluten-free flour
Powdered sugar, to dust on top

Directions:
- ➢ Set the oven's heat to 350°F. A 9.5 by 9.5-inch square baking pan should be butter-greased and placed aside.
- ➢ Combine the sugar and flour. Blend the butter into the flour until the mixture has a crumbly texture. Mix well after adding the water.
- ➢ Bake for 20 to 25 minutes after pressing into the pan's bottom.
- ➢ In a separate bowl, thoroughly combine the eggs, lemon juice, sugar, and flour. On top of the baked crust, pour.

- ➢ After 25 more minutes of baking, turn off the oven and let the food cool.

Nutrition: Calories: 212, Fat: 7.3g,
Carbohydrates: 35.1g, Protein: 3.4g.

Energy Bars

Cooking Time: x   **Servings:14**
Ingredients:
½ cup pumpkin seeds, roughly chopped
1 tbsp dark chocolate, chopped roughly
4 tbsp dried cranberries, chopped roughly
½ tsp ginger, ground
⅓ cup sunflower seed butter or peanut butter
6 tbsp maple syrup
1 ½ cups puffed rice
½ tsp cinnamon, ground

Directions:
- ➢ Use parchment paper to line a square baking tray.
- ➢ Over a medium heat, heat the butter and the syrup. Add the puffed rice, pumpkin seeds, dried cranberries, ginger, and cinnamon after the butter has melted. Evenly coat the components.
- ➢ Evenly spread the mixture throughout the pan, then cover it with a new piece of parchment paper and crush it with even pressure.
- ➢ After melting, drizzle the mixture with the dark chocolate. Cut after 2 hours in the refrigerator.

Nutrition: Calories: 121, Fat: 6.4g,
Carbohydrates: 14.4g, Protein: 3g.

Raspberry–chia Seed Ice Pops

Cooking Time: x   **Servings:6**
Ingredients:
½ cup water
1½ tablespoons chia seeds
6 ice-pop molds and handles
1½ cup raspberries (fresh or thawed frozen)
4 tablespoons sugar, divided
1 (15-ounce) can light coconut milk

Directions:
- ➢ Combine the raspberries, two tablespoons of water, and sugar in a food processor and blend until smooth.
- ➢ Fill each ice-pop mold with about 1 inch of the raspberry mixture and place in the freezer to harden (about 30 mins). Place the remaining raspberry mixture in the refrigerator.
- ➢ Whisk the coconut milk, the remaining two tablespoons of sugar, and the chia seeds in a small bowl.
- ➢ Add the coconut milk mixture to the ice-pop molds, distributing evenly. Freeze for another 30 minutes.
- ➢ Add the remaining raspberry mixture to the ice-pop molds, add the sticks or handles, and freeze for at least 4 hours, until completely frozen solid.

Nutrition: Calories: 115; Protein: 1g; Fat: 6g; Carbohydrates: 14g.

Deviled Eggs

Cooking Time: 0 Mins   **Servings:6**
Ingredients:
3 scallions, green parts only, minced
½ teaspoon sea salt
⅛ teaspoon freshly ground black pepper
½ teaspoon ground paprika
6 hardboiled eggs, peeled and halved lengthwise
½ cup Low-FODMAP Mayonnaise
2 tablespoons Dijon mustard

Directions:
- ➢ Separate the egg yolks carefully from the whites into a small bowl. Set aside the whites.
- ➢ Mash the yolks with a fork after adding the mayonnaise, mustard, scallions, salt, paprika, and pepper.
- ➢ Return the mixture to the egg whites with a spoon.

Nutrition: Calories: 240; Fat: 18g; Carbohydrates: 11g; Protein: 10g.

Macadamia–chocolate Chip Cookies

Cooking Time: x   **Servings: 20**
Ingredients:
⅔ cup (85 g) superfine white rice flour
½ cup (75 g) cornstarch
½ teaspoon baking soda
½ cup (95 g) chocolate chips
½ cup (70 g) roasted unsalted macadamia nuts, roughly chopped
¼ cup (20 g) soy flour
¼ cup (55 g) packed light brown sugar
¼ cup (55 g) superfine sugar
8 tablespoons (1 stick/120 g) unsalted butter, cut into cubes, at room temperature
1 large egg
1 teaspoon vanilla extract
Directions:
- ➢ Set the oven temperature to 325°F (170°C). Using parchment paper, line two baking pans.
- ➢ In a medium bowl, combine the brown sugar, butter, and superfine sugar. Using an electric hand mixer, whip the ingredients until thick and pale. Beat well after adding the egg and vanilla.
- ➢ Into a bowl, three times sift the rice flour, cornstarch, soy flour, and baking soda (or whisk in the bowl until well combined). Stir in the macadamia nuts and chocolate chips after adding to the butter mixture and thoroughly beating it.
- ➢ Leaving space for spreading, drop spoonful of dough onto the baking sheets. Until browned, bake for 10 to 15 minutes. After 5 minutes of cooling on the sheets, place on a wire rack to complete cooling.

Nutrition: Calories: 142; protein: 2g; Fat: 9g; carbohydrates: 16g.

Peanut Butter Cookies

Cooking Time: 10 Mins   **Servings:24**
Ingredients:
1 teaspoon baking soda
½ teaspoon vanilla extract
Pinch sea salt
1 cup sugar-free natural peanut butter
½ cup packed brown sugar
1 egg, beaten
Directions:
- Set the oven's heat to 350°F.
- Use clean parchment paper to line a baking sheet and set it aside.
- Combine the peanut butter and brown sugar in a medium bowl.
- After adding the salt, thoroughly mix in the egg, baking soda, vanilla, and salt. Twenty-four teaspoon-sized dough balls should be formed; place them on the prepared baking sheet. With a fork, lightly flatten in a crosshatch pattern.
- Bake the cookies for around 10 mins or until they completely puff up and turn golden brown.

Nutrition: Calories: 78; Fat: 6g; Carbohydrates: 5g; Protein: 3g

Coconut Rice Pudding

Cooking Time: x   **Servings:6**
Ingredients:
3 cups (750 ml) milk, lactose-free milk, or suitable plant-based milk (more if needed)
Heaping ¼ cup (20 g) shredded sweetened or unsweetened coconut
One 13.5-ounce (400 ml) can light coconut milk
2 teaspoons vanilla extract
1½ cups (300 g) Arborio rice
¾ cup (165 g) superfine sugar
Maple syrup, for serving (optional)

Directions:
- In a medium saucepan over moderate heat, add the sugar, milk, coconut milk, and vanilla. Stirring often, bring to a boil.
- Put the rice in. For about 50 minutes, reduce the heat and simmer the rice, stirring frequently, until the liquid has been absorbed and the rice is soft.

- If more milk is needed, add it.
- In the meantime, prepare a baking sheet with foil and preheat the oven to 325°F (170°C). When the coconut is just beginning to turn golden brown, sprinkle it evenly over the baking sheet and bake for 10 to 12 mins.
- Top the rice pudding with the toasted coconut and sprinkle it with maple syrup, if preferred, and serve it warm or at room temperature.

Nutrition: Calories: 417; protein: 9g; Fat: 7g; carbohydrates: 78g

Salted Caramel Pumpkin Seeds

Cooking Time: 25 Mins   **Servings:16**
Ingredients:
¼ tsp cinnamon, ground
1 ½ tbsp butter
1 tbsp white sugar
1 ½ tbsp brown sugar
½ tsp rock salt
½ tsp ginger, ground
Pinch of nutmeg
Roasted seeds
2 cups pumpkin seeds
2 ½ tbsp sugar
2 tsp water
Salted caramel sauce
Directions:
- Turn the oven on to 300°F.
- Combine the water, sugar, and pumpkin seeds. To help the sugar and spices stick, the seeds should be slightly moist.
- Grease and line a tray with parchment paper. After equally distributing the seeds across the baking sheet, bake for 25 minutes. The seeds ought to be crisp and golden. When cooking the seeds, don't forget to stir them halfway through.
- When the seeds are done baking, heat the butter in a clean skillet over medium heat. Butter should be combined with sugar and salt, then cooked for 2 minutes to a deep golden color.
- Reduce the heat. Returning the caramel to the tray after adding the seeds, let it cool.

Nutrition: Calories: 124, Fat: 9.8g, Carbohydrates: 5.7g.

Pineapple Salsa

Cooking Time: x   **Servings:2**
Ingredients:
½ teaspoon salt
Juice of 1 lime
1 tablespoon olive oil
2 cups chopped pineapple
2 jalapeño chiles, seeded and finely chopped
¼ cup finely chopped cilantro

Directions:
- ➢ In a medium bowl, add all the ingredients and toss thoroughly.
- ➢ To let the flavors to blend, let the food remain at room temperature for 15 to 20 minutes before serving.

Nutrition: Calories: 73; Protein: 1g; Fat: 4g; Carbohydrates: 11g

Chocolate Truffles

Cooking Time: x   **Servings:25**
Ingredients:
⅓ cup (80 ml) sweetened condensed milk
2 tablespoons rum or brandy (optional)
1½ cups (150 g) gluten-free chocolate sprinkles
7 ounces (200 g) gluten-free vanilla cookies, finely crushed (about 2 cups)
⅓ cup (35 g) unsweetened cocoa powder

Directions:

- ➢ In a medium dish, combine cocoa and the crumbled cookies. Form a firm dough using the condensed milk, rum (if using), and additional ingredients.
- ➢ Place the chocolate sprinkles in a bowl that is not too deep. With your hands, roll teaspoonfuls of the truffle mixture into balls.
- ➢ Add the chocolate sprinkles and toss to coat. Refrigerate until it becomes firm.

Nutrition: calories: 99; protein: 1g; Fat: 2g; carbohydrates: 20g

Kiwi Yogurt Freezer Bars

Cooking Time: 0 Mins   **Servings:6**
Ingredients:
Freezing: Overnight
½ cup lactose-free plain yogurt
4 packets stevia
2 cups unsweetened almond milk
4 kiwis, peeled and chopped

Directions:
- ➢ Combine the almond milk, kiwis, yogurt, and stevia in a blender. Process until smooth.
- ➢ Pour the mixture into six ice pop molds.
- ➢ Refrigerate overnight.

Nutrition: Calories:59; Fat: 2g; Carbohydrates: 10g; Protein: 2g

CHAPTER NINE

SOUP, SALAD AND SIDES

Peppered Beef And Citrus Salad

Cooking Time: x   **Servings:4**
Ingredients:
¼ cup (60 ml) fresh lemon juice
2 teaspoons olive oil
1 heaping tablespoon freshly ground black pepper, plus more for serving
1 orange, peeled and cut into segments
1 head butter lettuce (Boston or Bibb), leaves separated
1 pound (450 g) beef sirloin or top round steak
2 teaspoons garlic-infused olive oil
1 heaping tablespoon light brown sugar
Salt
One 8-ounce (225 g) can water chestnuts, drained and roughly chopped
Directions:
➢ In a clean frying pan over moderate heat, warm the olive oil. For medium-rare or the degree of doneness you choose, add the beef and cook it for 4 minutes on each side. After giving the meat 10 minutes to rest, slice it thinly.
➢ To prepare the marinade, whisk together in a medium bowl the garlic-infused oil, pepper, lemon juice, brown sugar, and salt to taste.
➢ When the meat is completely covered in the marinade, add it and mix. For 3 hours, cover and chill.
➢ In a sizable bowl, mix the steak, lettuce, water chestnuts, and any leftover marinade. Add several grinds of black pepper last, then serve right away.
Nutrition: calories: 369, protein: 23g, Fat: 23g, carbohydrates: 18g

Orange, Red, And Green Buckwheat Salad

Cooking Time: x   **Servings:4**
Ingredients:
1/4 cup extra-virgin olive oil
1/4 teaspoon sea salt
2 tablespoons no-sugar-added dried cranberries
2 cups arugula

2 cups mesclun greens
2 tablespoons maple syrup
2 tablespoons rice wine vinegar
1 tablespoon balsamic vinegar
2 cups buckwheat, cooked and rinsed
1/2 pound sweet potatoes, peeled, roasted and cubed
1/4 cup slivered almonds
Directions:
➢ Combine the extra-virgin olive oil, maple syrup, balsamic vinegar, rice wine vinegar, and salt in a small bowl to make the dressing. Place aside.
➢ Combine the buckwheat, sweet potatoes, cranberries, arugula, mesclun greens, and almonds in a sizable bowl.
➢ Sprinkle on the dressing and gently stir.
Nutrition: Calories: 447, Fat: 18g, Protein: 10g, Carbohydrates: 66g

Abundantly Happy Kale Salad

Cooking Time: x   **Servings:5**
Ingredients:
2 radishes, sliced very thin
1 cup sliced fennel bulb
1 cup fresh blueberries
1 cup shredded butter lettuce
1 medium stalk celery, diced
1 medium yellow bell pepper, seeded and diced
9 large leaves curly kale, thinly shredded (ribs and stems removed)
1/2 teaspoon sea salt
3 tablespoons extra-virgin olive oil, divided
Juice of 1 large lemon
1 medium carrot, peeled and grated
1 tablespoon hemp seeds
1 tablespoon pumpkin seeds
1 tablespoon chopped walnuts
2 cups shredded common (green) cabbage
Directions:
➢ Place the kale in a medium bowl and top with two tablespoons of oil and salt. Till the leaves start to darken and soften, rub the leaves with your hands.
➢ Gently whisk in the remaining ingredients and oil. For up to three days, keep sealed in the refrigerator.
Nutrition: Calories: 163, Fat: 11g, Protein: 4g, Carbohydrates: 17g

Chive Dip

Cooking Time:30 Mins   **Servings: 10**
Ingredients:
2 tbsp oil (best with onion-infused but can be substituted with other approved oils)
1 tsp lemon juice
2 tbsp parsley, fresh, chopped finely
1 cup mayonnaise
2 tbsp chives, dried
Pinch of salt

Directions:
- In a bowl, combine the mayonnaise, oil, chives, salt, and parsley.
- Add lemon juice or your preferred herbs.
- Allow to chill for 30 minutes in the refrigerator before serving with suggested fresh vegetables or chips.

Nutrition: Calories: 82, Fat: 7.8g, Carbs: 2.9g, Protein: 0.4g.

Chicken Noodle Soup with Bok Choy

Cooking Time: x   **Servings:4**
Ingredients:
3 bunches baby bok choy, leaves separated, rinsed and drained
½ cup (40 g) bean sprouts
2 teaspoons gluten-free soy sauce
1 pound (450 g) boneless, skinless chicken breasts, very thinly sliced
8 cups (2 liters) gluten-free, onion-free chicken or vegetable stock*
1 heaping tablespoon grated ginger
4 kaffir lime leaves
8 ounces (225 g) gluten-free rice vermicelli, broken into 2-inch (5 cm)
pieces

Directions:
- In a big, heavy-bottomed pot, combine the stock, ginger, and lime leaves, and boil.
- For five minutes, add the chicken, lower the heat, and simmer.
- Add the rice noodles, bok choy, and bean sprouts.

- Continue simmering for an additional 5 mins or until the noodles are soft.
- After removing the lime leaves and adding the soy sauce, immediately serve.

Nutrition: Calories: 362, protein: 31g, Fat: 2g, carbohydrates: 46g

Glorious Strawberry Salad

Cooking Time: x   **Servings:4**
Ingredients:
1/4 cup chopped fresh basil
2/3 cup extra-virgin olive oil
1/2 medium avocado, cut into eighths
1/2 cup crumbled goat cheese
1/4 teaspoon sea salt
6 cups fresh baby spinach
1/2 cup sliced strawberries
1/4 cup whole walnuts
1 tablespoon freshly ground black pepper
3 tablespoons rice wine vinegar

Directions:
1. In a large salad bowl toss together spinach, strawberries, walnuts,
basil, goat cheese, salt, and pepper.
2. In a small bowl whisk together vinegar and oil. Drizzle over salad and
toss salad again.
3. Serve on individual salad plates and top each with avocado.

Nutrition: Calories: 478, Fat: 48g, Protein: 6g, Carbohydrates: 8g.

Easy Fruit Salad

Cooking Time: 0 Mins   Servings:4

Ingredients:
1 pint fresh blueberries
2 bananas, sliced
6 clementines, sectioned
2 cups sliced fresh strawberries

Directions:
➢ Gently combine the clementines, strawberries, blueberries, and bananas in a large bowl.

Nutrition: Calories: 133, Fat: <1g, Carbohydrates: 34g, Protein: 2g

Turkey And Brown Rice Soup

Cooking Time: x   Servings:6

Ingredients:
1 medium red bell pepper, seeded and diced
1 bay leaf
2 tablespoons chopped fresh flat-leaf parsley
1/8 teaspoon sea salt
1/8 teaspoon freshly ground black pepper
6 cups Basic Roast Chicken Stock (see recipe in this chapter)
1 cup brown rice, rinsed
2 tablespoons extra-virgin olive oil
4 medium carrots, peeled and sliced into 1/4" rounds
1 (14.5-ounce) can of diced tomatoes
4 (3-ounce) turkey breast cutlets (uncooked), cut into 1" squares
5 cups baby spinach leaves

Directions:
➢ Prepare rice in a rice cooker or saucepan as directed on the package.
➢ In a stockpot, heat the olive oil over medium-high heat. Add the bay leaf, bell pepper, and carrots, then stir for five mins during sautéing.
➢ Fill the soup pot with stock, tomatoes, and turkey, then boil, reduce heat, cover, and simmer for 45 mins while stirring occasionally.
➢ Eliminate the bay leaf and toss in the spinach until it wilts.

➢ Turn off the heat. Add rice, parsley, salt, and pepper, and stir.

Nutrition: Calories: 345, Fat: 9g, Protein: 28g, Carbohydrates: 33g

Smoked Gouda And Tomato Sandwich

Cooking Time: 6 Mins   Servings:2

Ingredients:
⅔ cup grated smoked Gouda cheese, divided
1 tomato, cut into 6 slices
2 tablespoons garlic oil
4 slices gluten-free sandwich bread

Directions:
➢ A nonstick skillet is heated to medium-high heat.
➢ Apply the garlic oil on the outer surface of each slice of bread.
➢ Place two pieces of bread in the skillet oil-side down. Add three tomato slices and 1/3 cup cheese on top of each. Add the final two bread slices on top, oil side up.
➢ Cook the bread for 3 mins on each side until both sides are browned.

Nutrition: Calories: 536, Fat: 37g, Carbohydrates: 41g, Protein: 15g

Mashed Potatoes

Cooking Time:15 Mins   Servings: 14 (½ Cup Each)
Ingredients:
4 large Russet potatoes
1 tbsp rosemary, fresh, chopped
2 tbsp butter or margarine
2 tbsp olive oil
½ cup feta cheese
½ cup lactose-free milk
Pinch of salt

Directions:
➢ Cut the potatoes into cubes after washing and peeling them. Put them in a pot, then fill it with water. To allow evaporation, add a small amount of extra water.
➢ Cover the pot and boil the water.
➢ Lower the heat, remove the lid, and cook until the potatoes feel tender when poked with a fork.
➢ Pour the water out carefully, then leave the door open for five minutes.
➢ Chop the rosemary while the potatoes are cooking.
➢ Add the remaining ingredients to the saucepan after the five minutes have passed, excluding the salt and rosemary, and stir to combine until you reach the desired consistency.
➢ Add salt and rosemary to taste.
Nutrition: Calories: 106, Fat: 5g, Carbs: 11g, Protein: 3g.

Kale Sesame Salad with Tamari-ginger Dressing

Cooking Time: x   Servings:2
Ingredients:
1/4 medium avocado, sliced in half
11/2 tablespoons sesame seeds
4 cups shredded kale (thick ribs and stems removed)
1/2 cup peeled and julienned carrots
1 tablespoon rice wine vinegar
1/2 tablespoon finely grated gingerroot
1/2 tablespoon gluten-free soy sauce (tamari)
1 teaspoon lime juice
1/16 teaspoon wheat-free asafetida powder
3 tablespoons extra-virgin olive oil, divided

1 tablespoon chopped scallion, green part only
2 tablespoons chopped fresh basil
Directions:
➢ In a small skillet over moderate heat, then toast sesame seeds for approximately a minute or until they are golden brown. To prevent scorching of the seeds, stir continuously. Place aside.
➢ Fill a sizable salad dish with kale. Add one tablespoon of olive oil and massage the kale leaves with your hands until they are tender. Toss the carrots and scallion together.
➢ To make the dressing, combine the vinegar, ginger, soy sauce, lime juice, and asafetida in a small bowl.
➢ Drizzle the dressing over the leaves and give it one more swirl. Top each salad dish with a tablespoon of basil, a piece of avocado, and sesame seeds.
Nutrition: Calories: 344, Fat: 28g, Protein: 7g, Carbohydrates: 21g

Spinach And Bell Pepper Salad With Fried Tofu Puffs

Cooking Time: x   Servings:4
Ingredients:
¼ cup (55 g) packed light brown sugar
¼ cup (60 ml) sesame oil
14 ounces (400 g) fried tofu puffs, cut into cubes
⅓ cup (50 g) pine nuts
Salt and freshly ground black pepper
10½ ounces (300 g) baby spinach leaves (10 cups), rinsed and dried
¼ cup (60 ml) gluten-free soy sauce
¼ cup (60 ml) fresh lemon juice
1 tablespoon plus 1 teaspoon seasoned rice vinegar
1½ cups (75 g) snow pea shoots or bean sprouts
1 green bell pepper, seeded and sliced

Directions:
➢ In a small bowl, combine the sesame oil, lemon juice, soy sauce, vinegar, and brown sugar.
➢ In a sizable bowl, combine the spinach, snow pea shoots, bell pepper, tofu, and pine nuts. Add the dressing and drizzle, then quickly toss. Add salt and pepper before serving.
Nutrition: Calories: 571, protein: 24g, Fat: 40g, carbohydrates: 40g

Caramelized Fennel

Cooking Time: 60 Mins   **Servings:4**

Ingredients:

¼ cup freshly grated Parmesan

2 teaspoons lemon juice

2 tablespoons chopped fresh parsley

1 teaspoon lemon zest

¼ cup olive oil

4 large fennel bulbs, cut into ¼-inch-thick slices

1 teaspoon salt

Directions:

➢ Heat the olive oil over moderate heat in a large skillet.

➢ Fennel should be golden brown and very tender after 45 to 60 mins of cooking. If necessary, reduce the heat and continue cooking, stirring regularly.

➢ Add the cheese, parsley, lemon juice, and zest right before serving.

Nutrition: Calories: 228; Protein: 8g; Fat: 16g; Carbohydrates: 18g

Lentil Chili

Cooking Time: x   **Servings:4**

Ingredients:

1 large red bell pepper, seeded and chopped

3 Roma tomatoes, diced

1/4 cup chopped fresh cilantro

2 cups baby spinach

1/2 cup lactose-free sour cream (optional)

4 cups Vegetable Stock (see recipe in this chapter)

2 teaspoons chili powder

1 tablespoon olive oil

1 medium stalk celery, diced

1 large carrot, peeled and diced, or 1 cup store-bought shredded carrots

1 teaspoon ground cumin

2 cups canned lentils, drained and thoroughly rinsed

Directions:

➢ Add olive oil to a big saucepan that is already hot over moderate heat.

➢ Add the celery, carrot, and bell pepper; sauté for about 5 minutes, regularly stirring.

➢ Add 1/4 cup stock and stir.

➢ Stir in the cumin and chili powder; simmer for 1 minute.

➢ Add the remaining stock, tomatoes, cilantro, and lentils. Once boiling, lower the heat to medium-low, cover partially, and simmer for 25 minutes.

➢ Remove the top and cook for a further 8 minutes. Add spinach, stir, and cook for an additional two minutes.

➢ If using, garnish with sour cream and serve.

Nutrition: Calories: 236, Fat: 8g, Protein: 12g, Carbohydrates: 32g

Greens And Lemon Soup

Cooking Time:15 Mins   **Servings:4**

Ingredients:

2 tablespoons Garlic Oil

5 scallions, green parts only, chopped

5 cups stemmed, chopped Swiss chard

6 cups Low-FODMAP Vegetable Broth

½ teaspoon sea salt

¼ teaspoon freshly ground black pepper

Juice of 2 lemons

Directions:

➢ Heat the garlic oil in a large pot over moderate heat until shimmering.

➢ Add the chard and scallions. While stirring, cook for 3 minutes.

➢ Add the broth along with the salt and pepper. Cook for ten minutes with periodic stirring.

➢ Add the juice from one lemon.

Nutrition: Calories: 106, Fat: 7g, Carbohydrates: 11g, Protein: 2g

CHAPTER TEN

SAUCES, DRESSINGS
AND CONDIMENTS

Nutrition: Calories: 28, Fat: 0g, Protein: 0g, Carbohydrates: 5g

Salsa Verde

Cooking Time: x   **Servings: x**
Ingredients:
2 teaspoons capers, rinsed and drained
2 tablespoons fresh lemon juice, or to taste
Salt and freshly ground black pepper
1 tablespoon garlic-infused olive oil
2 handfuls of flat-leaf parsley, rinsed and dried
3 anchovy fillets in oil, drained (optional)
2 tablespoons olive oil

Directions:
➢ In a food processor or blender, add the parsley, anchovy fillets (if using), and capers. Process until thoroughly blended.
➢ Blend in the garlic-infused oil and olive oil gradually.
➢ Add the lemon juice along with a dash of salt and pepper.
➢ Transfer to a bowl or jar, cover, and keep chilled for up to five days.

Nutrition: calories: 53; protein: 1g; Fat: 5g; Carbohydrates: 1g.

Low-fodmap Mayonnaise

Cooking Time: 0 Mins   **Servings:1**
Ingredients:
¼ teaspoon sea salt
¾ cup extra-virgin olive oil
1 egg yolk
1 tablespoon red wine vinegar
½ teaspoon Dijon mustard

Directions:
➢ Blend or process the egg yolk with the vinegar, mustard, and salt for around 30 seconds.
➢ Scrape the sides of the blender jar or food processor bowl with a rubber spatula.
➢ Increase the blender or processor's speed to medium. Olive oil should be added very gradually, one drop at a time, as the food processor or blender is running.
➢ Keep the blender or processor running after roughly ten drops, then gradually trickle in the remaining olive oil until it is integrated and emulsified.
➢ The mayonnaise can be stored in the fridge for up to 5 days.

Nutrition: Calories: 169; Fat: 20g; Carbohydrates: <1g; Protein: <1g

Simple Brown Syrup

Cooking Time: x   **Servings:11**
Ingredients:
1 cup turbinado sugar
1 cup filtered water

Directions:
➢ In a saucepan, heat the water and sugar over low heat while frequently stirring until crystals dissolve.
➢ Remove from heat and allow it cool or reach room temperature before using.

Homemade Barbecue Sauce

Cooking Time: 10 Mins   **Servings:1**
Ingredients:
2 tablespoons Garlic Oil
1 teaspoon chili powder
½ teaspoon sea salt
⅛ teaspoon freshly ground black pepper
2 tablespoons tomato paste
6 scallions, green parts only, minced
½ cup apple cider vinegar
1 teaspoon liquid smoke
1 packet stevia

Directions:
➢ Mix all the necessary ingredients in a small pan over moderate heat.
➢ Simmer while stirring for 5 minutes.

Nutrition: Calories: 41; Fat: 4g; Carbohydrates: 2g; Protein: <1g

Garden Pesto

Cooking Time: x   **Servings:1**
Ingredients:
2 tablespoons Garlic-Infused Oil (see recipe in this chapter)
1/2 teaspoon sea salt
1/4 cup freshly grated Parmesan cheese
1/4 cup pine nuts, toasted
1 cup packed basil leaves
Directions:
➢ Place all the required ingredients in a food processor and blend until the mixture has the consistency of pesto.

Nutrition: Calories: 178, Fat: 17g, Protein: 5g, Carbohydrates: 2g

Garlic-infused Oil

Cooking Time: x   **Servings:1**
Ingredients:
4 garlic cloves, peeled, slightly smashed
1 cup plus 1 teaspoon grapeseed oil

Directions:
➢ Add garlic to a small pot of heated oil and cook for 10 minutes, stirring frequently.
➢ Remove from heat and allow the food cool fully.
➢ Take out the garlic and discard it, saving the oil.

Nutrition: Calories: 123, Fat: 14g, Protein: 0g, Carbohydrates: 0g

Pumpkin Seed Dressing

Cooking Time: x   **Servings:1**
Ingredients:
1/8 cup water
1 tablespoon finely chopped fresh cilantro
1 tablespoon fresh lemon juice
1/4 cup hulled green pumpkin seeds
1/16 teaspoon wheat-free asafetida powder
1/8 cup extra-virgin olive oil
1/4 teaspoon salt

Directions:
➢ In a small skillet over moderate heat, toast pumpkin seeds while tossing often until almost browned, about 5 minutes.
➢ Move to a platter to cool for two to three mins.
➢ Blend the remaining ingredients with the seeds to a smooth paste. Until smooth, blend. For 1-2 weeks, store in the refrigerator in an airtight container.

Nutrition: Calories: 109, Fat: 11g, Protein: 3g, Carbohydrates: 1g.

Maple Mustard Dipping Sauce

Cooking Time: x   **Servings:4**
Ingredients:
1 tablespoon pure maple syrup
1 tablespoon Dijon mustard
1 tablespoon light sour cream

Directions:
➢ Combine all the required ingredients in a small bowl and serve.

Nutrition: Calories: 20, Fat: 0g, Protein: 0g, Carbohydrates: 4g

Ginger Sesame Salad Dressing

Cooking Time:x   **Servings:1**
Ingredients:
2 tablespoons gluten-free soy sauce (tamari)
1" piece fresh gingerroot, minced
2 tablespoons demerara sugar
1 teaspoon sesame oil
1/2 cup extra-virgin olive oil
1/4 cup rice wine vinegar

Directions:
➢ Use a blender to thoroughly combine all ingredients.
➢ Dressing can be stored in the freezer for one week. Before serving, bring to room temperature.

Nutrition: Calories: 141, Fat: 14g, Protein: 0g, Carbohydrates: 4g

Low-fodmap Spicy Ketchup

Cooking Time: 20 Mins   **Servings:1**
Ingredients:
½ teaspoon ground ginger
½ teaspoon salt
¼ teaspoon freshly ground black pepper
¼ teaspoon cayenne
¼ teaspoon ground allspice

2 tablespoons Garlic Oil (here)
¼ cup tomato paste
¼ cup light-brown sugar
⅛ teaspoon ground cinnamon
⅛ teaspoon ground cloves
¼ cup red-wine vinegar
1 (15-ounce) can tomato sauce

Directions:
➢ In a small saucepan over moderate heat, warm the garlic oil. Cook the tomato paste for one min while stirring.
➢ Include the sugar and simmer, stirring constantly, until the sugar is completely dissolved.
➢ Add the allspice, cinnamon, ginger, cayenne, and cloves.
➢ Add the vinegar, salt, tomato sauce, and pepper by stirring. Cook for 15 to 20 mins, stirring periodically, or until the sauce is extremely thick.
➢ Allow to reach room temperature. Serve right away or keep chilled for up to a week in a closed container.

Nutrition: Calories: 28; Protein: 1g; Fat: 0g; Carbohydrates: 7g.

Artisanal Ketchup

Cooking Time: x   **Servings:3**
Ingredients:
1/4 teaspoon dried oregano
1/8 teaspoon ground cumin
Water (as needed)
1/8 teaspoon ground cinnamon
3/4 cup Tomato Paste
1 tablespoon white wine vinegar
1 tablespoon Simple Brown Syrup

Directions:
➢ In a food processor, blend all the ingredients and add water, 1/4 cup at a time.

Nutrition: Calories: 53, Fat: 2g, Protein: 1g, Carbohydrates: 8g

Basic Mayonnaise

Cooking Time: x   Servings:2
Ingredients:
2 tablespoons freshly squeezed lemon juice
1/4 teaspoon salt
2 large eggs
2 tablespoons Dijon mustard
11/3 cups safflower or sunflower oil
1/4 teaspoon freshly ground black pepper

Directions:
➢ Blend eggs and mustard in a food processor with the blade attachment. Process to achieve even blending.
➢ While the blender is still running, slowly stream in the oil and mix until mixed.
➢ Add the salt, pepper, and lemon juice, and pulse until smooth. If storing, put in the refrigerator for up to 3 days in a jar or container with a tight-fitting cover.

Nutrition: Calories: 86, Fat: 9g, Protein: 0g, Carbohydrates: 0g

Garlic Oil

Cooking Time: 5 Mins   Servings:1
Ingredients:
6 cloves garlic, sliced
1 cup olive oil

Directions:
➢ In a small saucepan over moderate heat, warm the olive oil.
➢ Add the garlic and cook for 5 minutes at a low simmer, stirring frequently.
➢ Pass a fine-mesh filter over the oil to remove the solids.
➢ Put the oil in the refrigerator for up to a week in a closed container.

Nutrition: Calories: 108; Protein: 0g; Fat: 13g; Carbohydrates: 0g

Cilantro-coconut Pesto

Cooking Time: x   Servings:1
Ingredients:
½ jalapeño, serrano, or Thai chile (optional)
Salt to taste
Juice of ½ lemon
1 tablespoon Garlic Oil (here)
1 bunch cilantro
6 tablespoons unsweetened shredded coconut
6 tablespoons toasted peanuts
1 tablespoon olive oil

Directions:
➢ Finely chop the cilantro in a food processor. Process to a paste after adding the coconut, peanuts, chile (if used), and lemon juice.
➢ Add the olive oil and garlic oil to the blender while it is running, and process until the desired texture is reached.
➢ Add extra oil, lemon juice, or water if the mixture is too thick. Salt should be added after tasting.

Nutrition: Calories: 90; Protein: 2g; Fat: 8g; Carbohydrates: 3g

Steakhouse Rub

Cooking Time: x   Servings:4
Ingredients:
1/2 teaspoon dried thyme
1/2 teaspoon dried rosemary, crumbled
1 teaspoon sea salt
1/4 teaspoon freshly ground black pepper
1/4 teaspoon maple sugar
1/2 teaspoon orange zest
1/4 teaspoon ground mustard

Directions:
➢ Combine all the required ingredients in a small bowl.

Nutrition: Calories: 2, Fat: 0g, Protein: 0g, Carbohydrates: 0g

Dill Dipping Sauce

Cooking Time: x   **Servings:3**
Ingredients:
7 ounces lactose-free sour cream
1/4 teaspoon salt
3 tablespoons chopped fresh dill
1 tablespoon lemon juice

Directions:
- Place all the required ingredients in a food processor and pulse until smooth.
- Use right away or put in an airtight jar and keep in the fridge for 3 to 4 days.

Nutrition: Calories: 64, Fat: 7g, Protein: 1g, Carbohydrates: 1g

Italian Vegetable Sauce

Cooking Time: x   **Servings:6**
Ingredients:
1/2 teaspoon ground dried ginger
1 pinch crushed red pepper
4 large carrots, peeled and cut into thin rounds
2 medium zucchini, quartered lengthwise and cut into 1/4" slices
1 (28-ounce) can whole tomatoes
1/8 teaspoon sea salt
1/8 teaspoon freshly ground black pepper
2 tablespoons extra-virgin olive oil
2 medium red bell peppers, seeded and diced
2 medium green bell peppers, seeded and diced
2 tablespoons demerara sugar
1 tablespoon dried basil
1 tablespoon dried oregano
1/2 teaspoon ground cinnamon

Directions:

- In a sizable stockpot, heat the olive oil over moderate heat. Bell peppers, carrots, and zucchini should be added to the pot and sautéed for about 10 minutes, turning constantly, until crisp-tender.
- Add the tomatoes, sugar, basil, oregano, cinnamon, ginger, crushed red pepper, salt, and black pepper. Break up the tomatoes with your hands.
- After bringing to a boil, simmer for 60 minutes uncovered.

Nutrition: Calories: 130, Fat: 5g, Protein: 3g, Carbohydrates: 21g

Macadamia Spinach Pesto

Cooking Time: 0 Mins   **Servings:1**
Ingredients:
½ cup grated Parmesan cheese
¼ cup Garlic Oil
2 cups fresh baby spinach
½ cup fresh basil leaves
¼ cup macadamia nuts
Zest of 1 lemon
½ teaspoon sea salt

Directions:
- Combine all the required ingredients in a food processor or blender.
- Continue processing until all ingredients are finely minced and blended.

Nutrition: Calories: 115; Fat: 12g; Carbohydrates: 1g; Protein: 3g

Teriyaki Sauce

Cooking Time: 5 Mins   **Servings:1**
Ingredients:
2 tablespoons mirin
1 tablespoon peeled and grated fresh ginger
1 tablespoon Garlic Oil
½ cup water
½ cup gluten-free soy sauce
¼ cup packed brown sugar

Directions:
➤ Combine all the required ingredients in a small pot set over medium-high heat.
➤ To thicken the sauce, simmer it for about 5 minutes while whisking.

Nutrition: Calories: 52; Fat: 2g; Carbohydrates: 8g; Protein: 2g

Stir-fry Sauce

Cooking Time: 0 Mins   **Servings:5**
Ingredients:
2 tablespoons cornstarch
Pinch red pepper flakes
1 tablespoon peeled and grated fresh ginger
¼ cup freshly squeezed orange juice
3 tablespoons gluten-free soy sauce

Directions:
➤ In a small bowl, combine the cornstarch, ginger, orange juice, soy sauce, and red pepper flakes.

Nutrition: Calories:33; Fat: <1g; Carbohydrates: 7g; Protein: 1g

Fiesta Salsa

Cooking Time:x   **Servings:6**
Ingredients:
1/4 teaspoon smoked paprika
1/4 teaspoon sea salt
1/2 teaspoon freshly ground black pepper
Juice of 1 medium lime
1/4 cup chopped green onions, green part only
1/4 cup chopped fresh cilantro
1/4 cup chopped fresh flat-leaf parsley
1 (10-ounce) can diced tomatoes, drained
1 (14.5-ounce) can diced tomatoes with green chilies
1 tablespoon garlic-infused extra-virgin olive oil
1/8 teaspoon wheat-free asafetida powder
1/4 teaspoon ground cumin
1/4 teaspoon coriander
1/4 teaspoon dried oregano

Directions:
➤ Fill a medium serving bowl with all the required ingredients. To blend, thoroughly stir.
➤ Store in the refrigerator for 5-7 days in an airtight container.

Nutrition: Calories: 46, Fat: 3g, Protein: 1g, Carbohydrates: 6g

Pepperonata Sauce

Cooking Time: x   **Servings:8**
Ingredients:
2 tablespoons Garlic-Infused Oil (see recipe in this chapter)
12 medium red, yellow, and green bell peppers, seeded and diced
1 tablespoon balsamic vinegar
1/8 teaspoon sea salt
1/8 teaspoon freshly ground pepper

Directions:
➤ In a big stockpot, heat oil over moderate heat.
➤ Add the peppers and cook for 5 mins. Stir in the vinegar, salt, and pepper.
➤ Decrease heat, cover, and simmer for 1 1/2-2 hours or until peppers are tender to the fork.

Nutrition: Calories: 87, Fat: 4g, Protein: 2g, Carbohydrates: 11g

Olive Tapenade

Cooking Time: 0 Mins   Servings:1
Ingredients:
1 cup chopped black olives
2 tablespoons Garlic Oil
2 tablespoons chopped fresh basil leaves
1 anchovy fillet, minced
1 tablespoon capers, chopped
Juice of ½ lemon
½ teaspoon sea salt
⅛ teaspoon freshly ground black pepper

Directions:
➢ Combine all the required ingredients in a
  small bowl and whisk thoroughly.

Nutrition: Calories: 61; Fat: 6g;
Carbohydrates: 2g; Protein: <1g

Pork Loin Rub

Cooking Time: x   Servings:1
Ingredients:
1 tablespoon sweet paprika
1 teaspoon dried oregano
1/2 teaspoon ground cumin
1 tablespoon sea salt
1 tablespoon demerara sugar
1 tablespoon ground cinnamon
1/2 teaspoon ground red pepper

Directions:
➢ Combine all the required ingredient in a
  small bowl.

Nutrition: Calories: 19, Fat: 0g, Protein: 0g,
Carbohydrates: 5g

CONCLUSION

In conclusion, the FODMAP diet is a valuable tool for managing gastrointestinal symptoms and improving overall digestive health. This book has provided a comprehensive guide to understanding and implementing the FODMAP diet successfully.

By grasping the concept of FODMAPs and their impact on the digestive system, readers have gained a deeper understanding of how certain foods can trigger uncomfortable symptoms. The low-FODMAP diet has been highlighted as an effective approach for symptom management, and readers have learned the importance of seeking guidance from a registered dietitian specializing in the FODMAP diet.

Throughout the chapters, practical tips and strategies have been shared to make the FODMAP diet more approachable and sustainable. From food recommendations and meal planning to navigating everyday challenges and dining out, readers now have the tools to put the low-FODMAP diet into practice.

It's important to emphasize that the FODMAP diet is not a one-size-fits-all approach, and patience is key when implementing it. It may take time to identify individual trigger foods and find the right balance of low-FODMAP and high-FODMAP foods that work best for each person. However, with the guidance of a registered dietitian and the information provided in this book, readers are equipped with the knowledge and support to navigate this journey successfully.

Remember, the goal of the FODMAP diet is to improve digestive symptoms and enhance quality of life. By being mindful of individual needs and preferences, and by seeking ongoing support and monitoring from a healthcare professional, readers can achieve a healthier gut and experience a significant improvement in their overall well-being.

With dedication, patience, and the knowledge gained from this book, readers are now empowered to take control of their digestive health and embark on a journey toward a more comfortable and fulfilling life.

INDEX OF RECIPES

Made in the USA
Las Vegas, NV
11 August 2023

75825742R10066